Also by Mark R. Levin

The Democrat Party Hates America

American Marxism

Unfreedom of the Press

Rediscovering Americanism

Plunder and Deceit

The Liberty Amendments

Ameritopia

Liberty and Tyranny

Rescuing Sprite

Men in Black

ON
POWER

MARK R. LEVIN

#1 *NEW YORK TIMES* BESTSELLING AUTHOR

THRESHOLD EDITIONS

New York   Amsterdam/Antwerp   London
Toronto   Sydney/Melbourne   New Delhi

Threshold Editions
An Imprint of Simon & Schuster, LLC
1230 Avenue of the Americas
New York, NY 10020

For more than 100 years, Simon & Schuster has championed authors and the stories they create. By respecting the copyright of an author's intellectual property, you enable Simon & Schuster and the author to continue publishing exceptional books for years to come. We thank you for supporting the author's copyright by purchasing an authorized edition of this book.

First Threshold Editions hardcover edition July 2025

THRESHOLD EDITIONS and colophon are trademarks of Simon & Schuster, LLC

Simon & Schuster strongly believes in freedom of expression and stands against censorship in all its forms. For more information, visit BooksBelong.com.

For information about special discounts for bulk purchases, please contact Simon & Schuster Special Sales at 1-866-506-1949 or business@simonandschuster.com.

The Simon & Schuster Speakers Bureau can bring authors to your live event. For more information, or to book an event, contact the Simon & Schuster Speakers Bureau at 1-866-248-3049 or visit our website at www.simonspeakers.com.

Interior design by Jaime Putorti

Manufactured in the United States of America

10   9   8   7   6   5   4   3   2   1

Library of Congress Control Number has been applied for.

ISBN 978-1-9821-4619-1
ISBN 978-1-9821-4621-4 (ebook)

For my family, friends, and fellow Americans

Contents

ON
POWER

1

ON POWER

Many have written about and debated the issue of power—including the ancients and modern philosophers, scholars, and statesmen alike. Why? Because power determines your social arrangements, quality of life, and, more to the point of this book, whether you are free or enslaved or some degree of either. In short, it determines your personal fate, the fate of your community, and the fate of a nation.

There are infinite ways to view power, innumerable contexts and circumstances in which to apply it. There is truly no simple, concise, all-purpose definition for what is meant by power. Clearly, however, it is more than a mere word. To spend time thinking, talking, or writing about it is not a mere abstraction, a useless amorphism, or an elitist esotericism. Power is a term meant to describe some kind of force or energy that surrounds us all the time, is both ubiquitous in your life and the life of the entire society, and is consequential in every way. Power is a core reality and characteristic of human existence. Yet without more to go on, such as context and circumstance, it can be ambiguous and elusive.

In all human pursuits, including personal pursuits and life events, power matters. At a macro level, power shapes economies, politics, and governments. Moreover, there are many variations: implied powers, necessary powers, assumed powers, granted powers, defined powers, limited powers, divided powers, ambiguous powers, seized powers, illegitimate powers, and more. For most people, these are unstated and often unnoticed or obscure kinds of power. But they exist and matter. Indeed, power is inextricably linked to liberty, although it is not to be confused with liberty itself. Power determines if there is too much liberty (e.g., anarchy) or too little (e.g., tyranny), depending on how power is exercised, who exercises it, and if it is bound by human rights.

The American Revolution is an important and obvious example of power properly pursued and exercised, the point of which was to promote individual and societal liberty, including by means of representative, limited, divided government—that is, ordered liberty. Conversely, autocrats of every stripe, and in all ages, have exploited liberty to empower themselves at the expense of the liberty of others. In fact, one's use of liberty this way, to expand one's own power to diminish if not denude the liberty of others, is, in a real sense, a paradox. And it is a cancer that apparently metastasizes over time within democracies. Of course, there are democracies that have lasted several centuries, but in the end, they have all succumbed to the steady increase in the centralization of power and a decline in individual and societal liberty. Sadly, this appears to be the nature of things. To be clear, then, even the most wisely conceived nation-states, mindful of man's abuse of power and established with the intent of curbing and restraining that power, seem to fail in the end. Gone are Athens, Rome, and numerous lesser societies. Democracies struggle against the centralization of power almost from the moment they are established.

History is replete with examples of tyrants grabbing power in the name of liberty. A prime example exists in Marxist regimes, where liberation through revolution—class warfare where the masses (the oppressed) are said to revolt against the powerful few (the oppressors)—and the promise of liberty through community and collectivism results in hellish, genocidal police states ruling over the people in their name but without their consent, and with an iron fist. Again, this is not only a phenomenon of tyrannies. As I noted on the back cover of my book *Liberty and Tyranny*, in our own country, President Abraham Lincoln observed that slave owners and abolitionists alike claimed to stand for liberty: "We all declare for liberty," said Lincoln, "but in using the same word we do not all mean the same thing. With some the word liberty may mean for each man to do as he pleases with himself, and the product of his labor; while with others, the same word may mean for some men to do as they please with other men, the product of other men's labor. Here are two, not only different, but incompatible things, called the same name—liberty. And it follows that each of the things is, by the respective parties, called by two different and incompatible names—liberty and tyranny."[1]

Like liberty in the context of power, *democracy* is another word that is used by the power-hungry to deceive and disarm. Indeed, I have already made several references to democracy, which can be loosely described as nonautocratic government. But democracy is often alluded to by those who reject it, as they reject universal, individual liberty and, where democracies exist, would destroy it. In his book *Politics and the English Language,* George Orwell writes about the perversion of "political words . . . used in a consciously dishonest way. That is, the person who uses them has his own private definition but allows his hearer to think he means something quite different."[2] "It is almost universally felt," writes Orwell, "that when we call a country democratic, we are praising it: consequently, the defenders of every kind of regime claim that it is a democracy, and fear that they might have to stop using the word if it were tied down to any one meaning."[3]

Thus, the word democracy, like the word liberty, is frequently used as a rhetorical weapon to deceive the true intentions and conceal the real nature of its abusers. Again, these behaviors and tactics are not exclusive to tyrants and autocracies. It is a real and growing threat in Western societies, as they increasingly centralize power in the name of unlimited egalitarian and so-called righteous causes— environmental justice, economic justice, social justice, equity, reparations, nationalized health care, the "existential threat of climate change," and so forth—which require and in fact demand the centralization of power to supposedly ameliorate the perceived, claimed, and in some cases manufactured societal maladies—the final resolutions of which are not only impossible, but also are not necessarily intended to be solvable. The agitations, demands, and related propaganda are sledgehammers with which to pummel the limited and divided institutional barriers to centralized power in democratic governments.

Let us narrow the focus. I start with the observation, which I believe is historically indisputable yet potentially controversial, and which you can infer from what I have already written, that over the millennia mankind has generally suffered more from the abuse of power and the concomitant diminution of liberty than from its humane and righteous application. There are important exceptions, of course, in the individual's everyday life and society generally. But narrowing the focus even further, in the long history of mankind, and even in modern times, the most pervasive form of governance, under which most human beings live and have lived, is authoritarian. Today, one need look only at the membership of the United Nations to prove the point. Some 70 percent of the world's population currently lives under brutal autocratic regimes.[4] This raises an unpleasant question: Is this the natural state of mankind, at least in the communal sense, even if individuals themselves wish for and seek liberty?* I term this *negative power*, which I will discuss more fully later in the book. That said, in a democracy negative power typically takes the form of a steadily increasing centralization of authority that starts slowly but eventually spreads more quickly to cover all corners of the nation, moving closer toward a quasi-autocratic model. It occurs primarily in three general ways: the imposition by the few (for example, the judiciary), the peaceful vote of the many (where the people willingly vote for their own demise), or the slow institutionalization of, and acquiescence to, as Thomas Hobbes characterized it, a leviathan (a dominating and domineering army of nonrepresentative bureaucrats).

Of course, there are degrees to which centralization develops and occurs, some more aggressive and ominous than others. Centralization in moderation, which is intended to secure liberty that does not exist or undergird existing liberty that is threatened or diminished by factionalism, mob rule, or anarchy, is of a different character than power secured for power's sake or with a tyrannical mind-set or purpose. Again, looking at our own history, in the early days of our republic,

---

* Philosopher Isaiah Berlin wrote of the "Two Concepts of Liberty"—positive and negative liberty—which I will also briefly address later. But it is not the same thing.

the Articles of Confederation were abandoned because the national government lacked the power to do much. As explained by the National Archives: "Just a few years after the Revolutionary War, James Madison, Alexander Hamilton, and George Washington feared their young country was on the brink of collapse. America's first constitution, the Articles of Confederation, gave the Confederation Congress the power to make rules and request funds from the states, but it had no enforcement powers, couldn't regulate commerce, or print money. The states' disputes over territory, war pensions, taxation, and trade threatened to tear the young country apart."[5]

Thus, the need for the Constitutional Convention and the birth of a new Constitution. I term this *positive power*, which I will explore later in the book. The Framers knew of both positive and negative power from, among other things, their own experiences with the British monarchy and their familiarity with the writings of ancient philosophers and contemporary revolutions (such as the French Revolution), that the centralization of governmental power, if not carefully and rightly designed, would destroy the new nation rather than serve its best interests.

Obviously, human beings are imperfect. This is not much of a revelation. Yet it seems downplayed or ignored by too many in democracies who acquiesce to or even cheer for governmental centralization when wrapped in promises of a larger welfare state, ethnic-racial-economic empowerment, or godlike fixes to natural disasters and climate events. However, the idea that the centralization of power—which necessarily concentrates authority in the hands of fewer imperfect individuals, and whose base of knowledge is naturally narrow—is a recipe for societal improvement, progress, stability, and well-being is not only counterintuitive but contrary to everyday human experience and mankind's history. Indeed, what makes these individuals more perfect as decision-makers, more moral as people, or more informed, wise, or prudential than anyone else? Nothing. Autocrats are not known to possess such qualities or demonstrate them when exercising power. Most excel at acquiring power, but not much else. Indeed, those who achieve such a station exhibit a greater affinity for the darker side of human behavior, including corruption, dishonesty, immorality, hubris, irrationality, anger, vainglory, egomania, bigotry, and so forth. Although a rare good or perceived benefit may come from their wielding of power, such as the claim that Italian fascist Benito Mussolini made the trains run on time (a myth), it is a farcical and often deadly delusion.

Moreover, where is the evidence that concentrated power in the hands of an administrative state, where the bureaucracy is to consist of specially trained experts and societal organizers who know what is best for the people and know how best to achieve those ends, has ever existed anywhere? Certainly not in America, as will be discussed later.

Contrarily, from Aristotle and Cicero to John Locke and Montesquieu and numerous others, philosophers and scholars have argued for the wisdom of diversified, dispersed, and mixed power within governments—that is, where power checks and balances power, which provides a greater likelihood of enlightened leadership and administration, greater respect and appreciation for the civil society and nongovernmental parts of society, and more protection of individual sovereignty and free will. In essence, a positive power structure attempts to contain and control the dark side of the human character and experience and emphasizes the capacity for a civilized, just society.

Again, in our country, the American Revolution and establishment of a republican government were intended to secure the traditions, customs, and values of the society, as concisely set forth in the Declaration of Independence—unlike the French Revolution, the purpose of which was to destroy the existing society, not only the ruling monarchy. Indeed, the Declaration is one of the most concise yet brilliant statements about humanity and society ever authored. This is not to say that other Western democracies lacked similar intentions. But America's purpose was known and declared before it was even a functioning country—that is, from the beginning. And its ultimate governmental design, the national Constitution, was a direct outgrowth of this purpose, not an imposition by an elite few, since the representatives of all the colonies participated in its development from the Constitutional Convention to the state ratification conventions.

When establishing our own national government, the debates among the delegates to the Constitutional Convention and, later, in the state ratifying conventions focused almost entirely on how to balance the necessity of centralized power, to secure the civil society and preserve individual liberty, with the recognition that in creating such an entity they risked imperiling the American experiment if the conferred power was not offset by competing powers. For the Framers, the answer was a mixed government. In essence, they adopted Locke's overarching governmental model of separating power and Montesquieu's more precise description of government divided between and among three entities—the legislative, executive, and judicial—each with relatively specific and distinct responsibilities, yet constantly competing with the others for power.

Montesquieu was the most widely read and cited philosopher during America's constitutional period. He is referred to directly in the Federalist Papers multiple times. In *The Spirit of the Laws*, Montesquieu explained that "[d]emocracy and aristocracy are not free states by their nature. Political liberty is found only in moderate governments. But it is not always in moderate states. It is present only when power is not abused, but it has eternally been observed that any man who has power is led to abuse it; he continues until he finds limits. Who would think it! *Even virtue has need of limits. So that one cannot abuse power, power must check power by the arrangement of things.* A constitution can be such that no one will be constrained to do the things the law does not oblige him to do or be kept from doing the things the law permits him to do."[6] (Italics added.)

Hundreds of years later, the late British Christian theologian, scholar, and author C. S. Lewis underscored Montesquieu's point about the abuse of power disguised as virtue. Lewis famously wrote:

Of all tyrannies, a tyranny exercised for the good of its victims may be the most oppressive. It may be better to live under robber barons than under omnipotent moral busybodies. The robber baron's cruelty may sometimes sleep, his cupidity may at some point be satiated; but those who torment us for our own good will torment us without end for they do so with the approval of their own conscience. They may be more likely to go to Heaven yet at the same time likelier to make a Hell of earth. Their very kindness stings with intolerable insult. To be "cured" against one's will and cured of states which we may not regard as disease is to be put on a level of those who have not yet reached the age of reason or those who never will; to be classed with infants, imbeciles, and domestic animals.[7]

Montesquieu further warned that should the distinct nature of these branches dissolve and transition from separation of powers to the concentration of powers, the result would be tyranny. "When legislative power is united with executive power in a single person or in a single body of the magistracy, there is no liberty, because one can fear that the same monarch or senate that makes tyrannical laws will execute them tyrannically. Nor is there liberty if the power of judging is not separate from the legislative power and from the executive power. If it were joined to legislative power, the power over the life and liberty of the citizens would be arbitrary, for the judge would be the legislator. If it were joined to executive power, the judge could have the force of an oppressor. All would be lost if the same man or the same body of principal men, either of nobles, or of the people, exercised these three powers: that of making the laws, that of executing public resolutions, and that of judging the crimes or the disputes of individuals."[8] Notice, too, Montesquieu's observation that tyranny is not unique solely to despots but is also to be feared in the form of groups, bodies, and mobs—even legislatures.

As the state conventions were debating whether to ratify the proposed Constitution, in *Federalist* No. 51, James Madison, considered the father of the document, echoed Montesquieu when he wrote: "*Human beings are imperfect and ambitious, so we need a government structure that guards against abuses of power.* Ambition must be made to counteract ambition. The interest of the man must be connected with the constitutional rights of the place. It may be a reflection on human nature, that such devices should be necessary to control the abuses of government. But what is government itself, but the greatest of all reflections on human nature? If men were angels, no government would be necessary. If angels were to govern men, neither external nor internal controls on government would be necessary. In framing a government which is to be administered by men over men, the great difficulty lies in this: you must first enable the government to control the governed; and in the next place oblige it to control itself."[9]

So much in life orbits around this word, idea, belief— *power*. And most of the discussion, to the extent it exists at all in an honest or coherent fashion, is in the form of generalities, sloganeering, demagoguery, and the like, used by politicians, media, ideologues, and academicians to manipulate, confound, and deceive—in which case power is used to control thought, discussion, and language. This book is intended to provoke a better comprehension of what is meant by power, its impact on the individual and mankind generally, and to stimulate a broader examination and dialogue about its applications. In doing so, and if it succeeds even modestly, perhaps it will prove an additional source for liberty and against tyranny.

2

ON NEGATIVE POWER

Negative power is power that is exercised by force or other less obvious coercive means. Among its purposes is to limit individual identity, sovereignty, and liberty. In its most aggressive form, and when exercised by a faction, cabal, or government, both autocratic and authoritarian—for example, Communist regimes, fascist regimes, terrorist quasi-states, etc.—the people are treated as servants to the proclaimed cause and those exercising power rather than the other way around. Its purpose is to devour and control society, not serve it. Consequently, it must denude individuals of their free will, self-worth, aspirations, development, progress, and human spirit and control the society generally through the exercise of concentrated, centralized, unchallenged, and ubiquitous power. It is critical to restrict speech and debate, manipulate language, and manufacture new meanings for existing words and new words with self-serving meanings. Propaganda and repetition are the mainstay controlling communication, and the pursuit of ideas, information, and knowledge is condemned and punished—that is, to dictate thought. Conformity, predictability, regurgitation, and obedience are crucial to the lifeblood of the despotic regime. The goal is to create vigorous followers and fanatics for the cause and the regime, not a healthy and robust society of self-sufficient, curious, freethinking, independent human beings.

Naturally, negative power is unmoored from the values and ideals born of the Bible, Reformation, and Enlightenment. It promotes that which is primitive and often barbaric. In governments born of and ruled through negative power, the legitimacy of the government and the way power is executed are without lament or moral and rational circumspection. There is a frightening callousness in the mind-set of the rulers and a cold-blooded brutality to their rule. Unlike John Locke's view of the social contract, where individuals voluntarily join and form a civil society with just laws, security, moral order, and the like, the individual is little more than a slave to the cause or the regime. People are collectively sheep to be herded in one direction or another, at the behest of and for the benefit of those exercising negative power.

But negative power need not be exercised, or present itself, in such aggressive forms. For modern Western societies, most of which are said to be advanced, enlightened, and democratic, negative power is more opaque—or what I call *soft* negative power. Typically, Western institutions have been established gradually, by experience and practice, or constituted by design, to counter or limit the most aggressive forms of negative power, such as dictatorships or oligarchies. However, over time they tend to become susceptible to a softer form of negative power. Political parties and political movements in the West look for advantages in acquiring, holding, and expanding their power, whether changing election laws, governing increasingly through nonrepresentative bureaucracies and so-called independent agencies and commissions, the rule of carefully selected judges or judicial councils, and the like. The conflict between honoring and complying with the institutional limits placed on power and the allure of self-aggrandizement is both real and perhaps inevitable over time. As such, the once authentic and thought-to-be effective institutions for limiting excesses of power are transformed into Potemkin-like fictions used to disguise the true intentions of the abusers and, worse, are transformed into tools in support of the exercise of soft negative power. This is *authoritarian democracy*.

Authoritarian democracy is when a democracy begins the slide into a form of authoritarianism, not all at once but steadily, where authoritarian attributes slowly proliferate, and one branch of the democracy begins to envelop the others, or where all branches coalesce into a whole. Either way, the exercise of power is steadily centralized and the citizenry increasingly peripheral. As I will discuss later, it typically results in rule by the unelected governmental branches—that is, the judiciary and the administrative state—but can also mutate into excessive executive or legislative empowerment.

Authoritarian democracies adopt and use the tactics of authoritarian regimes, albeit at first with more of a glove than an iron fist, but the underlying attributes are there. For example, legislatures that pass tyrannical laws, but which laws are said to be legitimate simply because the legislature adopted them; courts that disregard due process, but which trials are said to do justice because they were held in a court of law with defense counsel and juries present, etc. The use of law is said to be a legitimate application of power because it is the law, not because it is a proper, just, or moral law.

Even today, the impact of authoritarian democracy has seeped into our society's psyche so successfully that the late Austrian American economist Ludwig von Mises observed that one of the worst tyrannies of all, Marxism, has become part of the West's psyche: "To a considerable extent," wrote Mises, "without knowing it, many people are philosophical Marxists, although they use different names for their philosophical ideas."[1]

However, there are also those, perhaps many, who benefit from the government's use of soft negative power, including when that power is used, for example, to forcibly redistribute the wealth and property of those who produced and earned it for the use and enrichment of others, beyond the usual and basic needs of a civil society, and justify what would otherwise be considered thievery as noble and even moral. The beneficiaries of such soft negative power are fully aware that they did not earn what they have received but delude themselves in various ways that they are deserving of it.

Democracies have the seeds of their own destruction within them. Indeed, today soft negative power is ascendant—that is, the West, which obviously includes the United States, is regressing toward the more primitive way of thinking and governing and the more aggressive form of negative power. The circle of liberty and security surrounding each individual is shrinking as the supposed "common good" and "public interest," defined and determined by a relative handful of masterminds and politicians, is said to be increasingly imperative and paramount. The assumed legitimacy for interference in the individual's life has become so routine, assumed to be both necessary and inevitable, that their justifications are less important. The growth of centralized government and its attendant authority are presented as, and indeed seen by many as, predestined. Even essential to human and societal progress.

In America—a constitutional republic that built barriers, checks and balances, and the separation of powers within the construct of the national government and between and among the national government and the state and local governments—the Constitution was established for the explicit intent of defending against the failed experiences of past republics, such as Athens and Rome, as well as the tyranny of the monarchy, such as Britain, or the mob, such as the French Revolution. Nonetheless, even the best minds, armed with the most noble and prudent of purposes, and informed by history, philosophy, and experience, are unlikely to birth a republic forever safe from the relentless manipulation, deceit, and plotting of tyrannical minds and forces. The threat from within is real and always present. I wish it were not so, but experience and history point otherwise.

I realize what follows will be dismissed or castigated by certain partisans and fanatics. But that is to be expected, since my observations involve them, and they are not laudatory. In truth, among the most dangerous domestic menaces to present-day America is the Democrat Party. It is a political institution that exists for the purpose of agitating for and, in fact, breaching the Constitution's firewalls in pursuit of the ever-elusive earthly utopia. It is home to, among others, a conglomeration of Marxist, socialist, and Islamist ideologues and activists. Of course, this is not to say that the majority of its membership shares these ideologies. However, the majority of its membership does not rule the party.

I say this not as hyperbole for partisan political purposes, but as an everyday witness with functioning eyes and ears, reading and hearing the daily barrage of declarations and promises about the "fundamental transformation of America" and the dogged assault on America's foundations by its academics, Democrat Party apparatchiks, and surrogates. Indeed, unlike reform, the fundamental transformation of which they speak is the wholesale transmutation of a nation's character and traditions.

Moreover, the extensive written history of the cunningly named progressive movement unapologetically declares its purpose, as does its modern progeny in a flood of essays, books, and speeches, to fundamentally transform America. It is a force and presence in the United States, as it is in all Western democracies, albeit operating under different party and official nomenclatures, where truly enlightened progress is met with regressive and primitive ideological forces hailed as modern and futuristic. Thus, tearing down the barriers to centralized decision-making and governmental power and diminishing individual freedom to reengineer society and, indeed, mankind, are essential objectives, if not the epitome of both soft negative power and negative power.

This is precisely why the early progressive intellectuals in America in the late 1800s and early 1900s, including future Democrat president Woodrow Wilson, relentlessly and furiously assailed both the Declaration of Independence and the Constitution—especially separation of powers and federalism. Wilson wrote about the need for a living and breathing constitution and insisted it be understood within an allegory to the human body. How, Wilson asked, can a person live if his organs are constantly working against each other rather than in harmony? In other words, separation of powers, the heart of the Constitution, is as deadly to America as the separation of organs in the human body would be.

Moreover, Wilson and his progressive contemporaries argued that successive generations are not bound by the decisions and doctrines of the past, and we need not adhere to them, any more than the authors of the Declaration and Constitution were bound by those who preceded them. We are free to do as we wish, just as they were, and we need not worship them or what they wrote.[2]

Wilson and his ilk argued for a sinister revolution, indeed launched that revolution, in which intellectual elites and self-appointed experts, through a ruling class of like-minded manipulators and schemers, social engineers, and contrivers, would employ the instrumentalities of the unelected and nonrepresentative parts of the federal government and further empower them, in service to the cause of the so-called new progressivism—a form of European totalitarianism—that I have previously termed American Marxism. In this way, the Constitution could be altered if not bypassed, with the topdown imposition of life-altering directives, regulations, and ultimatums to accomplish their ends. The will of the people through actual representative bodies is to be adhered to only when convenient and aligned with the ruling class's causes and goals. Otherwise, it is to be circumvented, killed through delay and atrophy, or, where feasible, simply ignored.

Wilson and others insisted that a complete break from the past is required, a blank slate upon which to design this new governing blueprint. In this they were mimicking Karl Marx. At first Wilson could not decide if this was best accomplished through an all-powerful president or judiciary. But he eventually settled on what he considered the most obvious and certain means by which to accomplish this outcome—the *judiciary*. What better means to achieve the progressive ends, he believed, than the careful selection and appointment of ideological soul mates, who serve for life and without any effective method for public accountability, who would drive this revolution and give it a legal pretext, justification, authority, and protection? Indeed, if your objective is the fundamental transformation of constitutional republics and parliamentary democracies into centralized leviathans, the path of least resistance and maximum impact would seem to be the judiciary.*

---

* I use the words *democracy* and *republic* interchangeably for the purposes of this book and brevity. Of course, there are significant differences between them.

The entire premise for this revolution is not, for example, as Marx and others predicted and hoped, to foment a bottom-up movement—that is, the oppressed proletariat overthrowing the oppressor bourgeoisie. For in much of the Western world, and certainly in America, the public do not seek such a violent revolution. In fact, in America and elsewhere, there is no popular will to overthrow the existing society and, on the contrary, the people have and are prepared to fight and die for their country.

Thus, out of necessity was born, at the hands of the progressive masterminds, a different kind of bourgeoisie, if you will, not strictly or even primarily defined by economic classifications, but driven by the accumulation of power and built on authoritarian impulses and objectives. A ruling class with more power than the Constitution authorizes. It was and is essential, therefore, that the stable, predictable, and just governing laws undergirding the existing society, starting in America with the Constitution itself, which are both foundational and celebrated by the citizenry, be recast as their opposite—unjust, immoral, dehumanizing, etc. The status quo must be usurped in small ways and large. Consequentially, the public, most of whom are unaware of the creeping transition, acquiesce to it, and are even convinced to celebrate it as progress, is exposed to the vagaries of rulers and the threats and control of a rising police state.

As such, the civil society, the forerunner and vanguard of a just body politic, commonwealth, and ultimately, democratic government cannot last long as it lay naked for the power-hungry to take advantage. Indeed, the law is, at bottom, the exercise of power—and in this case, the exercise of negative power. Consequently, insinuating revolutionaries into the judiciary, as Wilson and others preached as a priority, is the surest way to achieve such ends.

Today, the Democrat Party's designs on the independence of the Supreme Court, including increasing its numbers to install additional handpicked ideologues who share its revulsion of constitutional constraints and limitations, a.k.a. activist judges and justices, is just one of many examples—albeit the gravest in this moment—of what I will call the *deconstitutionalization* of America. Inasmuch as the law is about the distribution and application of power, fundamentally the Constitution constrains the power of the power-hungry and, therefore, is its target.

Israel is a prime example of a judicial tyranny—a nation that is run by a relative handful of lawyers sitting as Supreme Court justices. The cancer of judicial tyranny has metastasized to the point where its government can no longer be legitimately or accurately described as a parliamentary democracy. Israel was established without a constitution or like system. This is the crack through which its Supreme Court seized for itself the power to essentially make the nation's laws and supplant the elected governmental branches. Separation of powers is a fiction. The court is a power unto itself with literally no bounds. It always has a say, if it chooses, on matters wholly legislative or executive, and its say is final. In essence, Israel's highest court sits as an oligarchy or, perhaps more accurately, an ideological politburo, high above all governmental and societal institutions, where it even selects many of its own members and whatever issues it wishes to adjudicate.

As legal scholar and retired federal appellate judge Richard Posner has written: "Among the rules of law" that Israel's Supreme Court has created "are . . . that judges cannot be removed by the legislature, but only by other judges; that any citizen can ask a court to block illegal action by a government official, even if the citizen is not personally affected by it (or lacks 'standing' to sue, in the American sense); that any government action that is 'unreasonable' is illegal ('put simply, the executive must act reasonably, for an unreasonable act is an unlawful act'); that a court can forbid the government to appoint an official who had committed a crime (even though he had been pardoned) or is otherwise ethically challenged, and can order the dismissal of a cabinet minister because he faces criminal proceedings; that in the name of 'human dignity' a court can compel the government to alleviate homelessness and poverty and that a court can countermand military orders, decide 'whether to prevent the release of a terrorist within the framework of a political 'package deal,' and direct the government to move the security wall that keeps suicide bombers from entering Israel from the West Bank."[3] "[O]nly in Israel (as far as I know) do judges confer the power of abstract review on themselves, without benefit of a constitutional or legislative provision."[4]

Israel can be more accurately described as a judicial oligarchy rather than a healthy, functioning democracy. Incredibly, reform efforts by Israel's elected parliament, the Knesset, to modestly rein in the judiciary have been overruled by the Supreme Court itself. Hence, there are no effective means for the public, through its elected representatives, to lawfully change the course of their government. And apparently, at least for a riotous minority of the citizenry on the political left, and for whom the Supreme Court delivers policy results, the tyranny of the judiciary is the means that justifies the ends.

However, it would be wrong to assume that soft negative power exists only in the realm of the unelected. In addition to the usurpation of the judiciary, the pursuit of authoritarian aims, at least in a republic or democracy, particularly one that is relatively satisfied with existing societal norms and conditions, is also easier and likelier achieved by softening up the citizenry and gradually disarming the people and inculcating them with state-run propaganda, ideas, values, and objectives. That is, without the blunt force of more aggressive power and in a manner and mode more subtle and suitable to a public experienced in democratic principles. Consequently, the election process, and the elective governmental entities, provide the patina of a free and open society and participatory government where the individual is said to have a real role in governmental decision-making and outcomes and believes it to be so, but in fact is increasingly more a rote routine—at least that is a necessary intent if not effect of soft negative power.

For example, in America, Congress has created a budgetary device known as the omnibus bill. These bills are thousands of pages in length, laced with unrelated and diverse budget and spending matters, the language of which is complicated and intricate. The ruling class, its bureaucrats, lobbyists, special interests, and lawyers trained to interpret the language—if they did not write it in the first place—are able to determine spending priorities involving trillions of dollars in public money without the citizenry having a clue, let alone any effective input. Given the ubiquity of the federal government and its reach into virtually all areas of society, this is an enormous betrayal of representative government by the supposed representative branches.

Indeed, the elected branches have engaged in a century-long building project, the construction of a massive administrative state, the contours of which are elusive and seemingly boundless, and constructed without a constitutional foundation. Nonetheless, the judiciary has ruled otherwise and magically anointed this manufactured fourth branch of government with the appearance of legitimacy—for the purpose of shifting away from a representative republic to a centralized yet pervasive ministerial class reporting directly to and serving the interests of the ruling class. The delegation of representative government to a nonrepresentative, ever-expanding bureaucratic behemoth is, by intent and design, the overthrow of actual representative and consensual government. As a result, the unelected judiciary and bureaucracy hold enormous power over the people by literally removing their participation and consent.

In his book *Democracy in America*, Alexis de Tocqueville, the renowned French political scientist and historian who traveled throughout America, presciently wrote in 1840 what he believed could be America's downfall as a democracy—a massive administrative state. He explained, in part:

> Above this race of men stands an immense and
> tutelary power, which takes upon itself alone to
> secure their gratifications and to watch over their
> fate. That power is absolute, minute, regular,
> provident, and mild. It would be like the authority
> of a parent if, like that authority, its object was
> to prepare men for manhood, but it seeks, on the
> contrary, to keep them in perpetual childhood;
> it is well content that the people should rejoice,
> provided they think of nothing but rejoicing.
> For their happiness such a government willingly
> labors, but it chooses to be the sole agent and the
> only arbiter of that happiness; it provides for their
> security, foresees and supplies their necessities,

facilitates their pleasures, manages their principal
concerns, directs their industry, regulates
the descent of property, and subdivides their
inheritances. What remains, but to spare them all
the care of thinking and all the trouble of living?[5]

Thus it every day renders the exercise of the
free agency of man less useful and less frequent,
it circumscribes the will within a narrower
range and gradually robs a man of all the uses of
himself. The principle of equality has prepared
men for these things; it has predisposed men
to endure them and often to look on them
as benefits.[6]

After having thus successively taken each
member of the community in its powerful grasp
and fashioned him at will, the supreme power
then extends its arm over the whole community.
It covers the surface of society with a network of
small, complicated rules, minute and uniform,
through which the most original minds and
the most energetic characters cannot penetrate,
to rise above the crowd. The will of man is
not shattered, but softened, bent, and guided;

men are seldom forced by it to act, but they are constantly restrained from acting. Such a power does not destroy, but it prevents existence; it does not tyrannize, but it compresses, enervates, extinguishes, and stupefies a people, till each nation is reduced to nothing better than a flock of timid and industrious animals, of which the government is the shepherd.[7]

I have always thought that servitude of the regular, quiet, and gentle kind which I have just described might be combined more easily than is commonly believed with some of the outward forms of freedom, and that it might even establish itself under the wing of the sovereignty of the people.[8]

In Europe, the situation is even graver. Parliaments, like America's Congress, have built immense bureaucracies through openly socialist economic policies dating back more than half a century. Again, these serve as substitutes for representative government as well. But layered atop these edifices, European governments have added multinational arrangements where each country's government has voluntarily and willingly surrendered significant aspects of their own national sovereignty and, in turn, their citizenry's sovereignty, to a collective of European countries under the establishment of another supergovernment. Specifically, the European Union (EU) is a supranational organization of twenty-seven countries, with each country ceding certain economic, legal, and governing authorities to the union. Each member country votes on policies that affect the other member nations.[9] Hence, an international governmental sovereign stands above the national governmental sovereign, a hierarchy of negative power. The severity of this governmental arrangement is intended to erode if not smother any serious or effective connection between the top-tier ruling class, made up of international elites, and the citizenry of a member nation, who are at the lowest level of the power tier. True participatory and representative government is a mockery, as the circle of liberty surrounding the individual is squeezed tighter without any practical or adequate recourse. This is authoritarian democracy.

How long can such governmental enterprises be sustained? So long as they are able to contain and restrain the human spirit and initiative, cage the civil society, and exert increasingly aggressive forms of negative power over the population. Indeed, the paranoid or threatened ruling class's instinct is for more repression and coercion, where civil liberties retract as the impulse for more control and survival kicks in. Authoritarian democracies become more authoritarian and less democratic.

I have made the argument that negative power exists in both open and closed societies, the former experiencing soft negative power. And it is in the ascendency today in most democracies, including in America. It takes different forms and moves at different paces.

The order of things—nature, morality, values, beliefs, etc.—precedes government, exceeds the earthly limits of government, and exists in perpetuity, in spirit if not reality, unlike any government. Indeed, all governments come and go over the course of human history. One group of men telling other men what to do, how to do it, and when to do it is by itself nothing more than men placing limits on other men. But in their essence, human beings are not beings of other men or governments. They are not creatures of the ruling class. There is a universe that is greater than and beyond mankind and government. There is an inherent and supreme law that is unamendable by man-made law. Only governments that are established and exist based on this universal order of things are, therefore, valid, legitimate, and right.

Conversely, as America's Founders repeatedly declared, legitimate government is not possible, let alone sustainable, if the citizenry is not virtuous. John Adams stated: "Our Constitution was made only for a moral and religious People. It is wholly inadequate to the government of any other."[10] George Washington agreed: "It is substantially true that virtue or morality is a necessary spring of popular government."[11] James Madison warned: "To suppose any form of government will secure liberty or happiness without virtue in the people is a chimerical idea."[12] This was the consensus view of the Founders.

Of course, soft negative power will always exist, even if no government exists. It will exist in the civil society and throughout private life, where laws, rules, or customs of some kind, generated from some source within a group or larger community, are established and must be established (formally or informally), and must be honored and enforced, to prevent chaos and anarchy, create some kind of social order, protect the individual and individual liberty, and secure the individual's holdings. Again, Locke called this a social contract. Consequently, some degree of soft negative power will be exercised that proscribes if not conscribes some level of individual liberty. It follows, therefore, that the same notion of soft negative power applies to the most beneficent and sound governments. But is this really or accurately characterized as soft negative power?

I began this chapter by positing that "[n]egative power is power that is exercised by force or other less obvious coercive means. Among its purposes is to limit individual sovereignty and liberty." But when negative power or, here, soft negative power, is exercised to *preserve* individual sovereignty and dignity and *nurture* the civil society—that is, when it has as its overall and fundamental purpose the *opposite* of the ultimate purpose of negative power, it is in use and intent a form of positive power.

From here we are ready to explore *positive power*.

3

ON POSITIVE POWER

Positive power starts from an altogether different premise than negative power. God is the sovereign. And through God, his children—that is, the individual and the people— are sovereign. Thus, power properly understood and exercised, in the context of government, is about the well-being of the people, not the rulers. The people are the sovereign, not the governing authority, and importantly, the belief in God-given eternal truths, natural law, and unalienable rights is the basis of a moral and virtuous society that transcends any ruling class.

One's approach to life and role in society and more involves practices, decisions, values, and beliefs that together form one's life philosophy, which results from learned, cognitive, reactionary, experiential, or even instinctive thought processes—and, significantly, faith. Faith is a vital if not the imperative influence in the life of the individual, a nation, and even in countries that are said to be secular and that formally or institutionally disclaim and seek to invalidate faith, including by indoctrination and force. And, of course, faith as preached and practiced by certain religions or religious leaders, now and in the past, has been used by despots and despotic regimes as other autocrats use power—power, to brutalize, destroy, and kill.

You may ask: How can faith be both pivotal to positive power yet a potential tool for negative power? Thus, further inquiry is crucial.

Let us begin with America's Declaration of Independence. It appeals to "the Laws of Nature and of Nature's God" and states, "We hold these truths to be self-evident, that all men are created equal, that they are endowed by their Creator with certain unalienable Rights, that among these are Life, Liberty and the pursuit of Happiness."

The Founders were men of science, reason, and experience, but they were also men of faith who worshipped God. Even among the Deists, namely Benjamin Franklin and Thomas Jefferson, they knew and professed the importance of faith in society and the establishment of the American republic.

As I explained in *Liberty and Tyranny*: "Reason cannot, by itself, explain why there is reason. Science cannot, by itself, explain why there is science. Man's discovery and application of science are products of reason. Reason and science can explain the existence of matter, but they cannot explain why there is matter. They can explain the existence of the universe, but cannot explain why there is a universe. They can explain the existence of nature and the laws of physics, but they cannot explain why there is nature and the laws of physics. They can explain the existence of life, but they cannot explain why there is life. They can explain the existence of consciousness, but they cannot explain why there is consciousness."[1]

The Founders did not believe they owed their origin to men and through men, but to a transcendent provenance— that is, to a higher source than man. God. Faith was fundamental to America's founding. Indeed, Christianity was and is our nation's dominant religion. Moreover, without Judaism there would be no Christianity. Together, Judeo-Christian values and beliefs redounded throughout our society from the earliest days of the colonists and still do today.

One layperson put it this way: "Judaism and Christianity have significantly influenced Western civilization. Their teachings have shaped ethical frameworks, legal systems, and cultural norms. The values derived from both faiths are evident in literature, art, and philosophy throughout history. Concepts like human rights, social justice, and the dignity of life are rooted in their teachings. Both religions advocate for compassion and moral integrity, impacting societal values. Their contributions extend beyond religious spheres, informing the development of Western thought and culture. . . ."[2]

As America became a nation of united states, it was never intended to be nor would it ever become a fundamentalist religious state or theocracy, as one sees throughout the Muslim world and elsewhere. It was never to be a repressive religious state that smothers alternative religious beliefs or a state that punished or silenced nonbelievers, atheists, or agnostics. On the contrary. Early on, religious tests and requirements that existed in some of the colonies would quickly disappear. Among other reasons, Judaism and Christianity do not seek to compel, let alone demand doctrinal purity.

The United States is among the most religiously tolerant nations on earth. In fact, it matters not at all what one does or does not believe to enjoy the freedoms and security that American society offers, and which are explicitly protected by the Constitution. The first sentence of the First

Amendment declares: "Congress shall make no law respecting an establishment of religion, or prohibiting the free exercise thereof. . . ."[3]

The reason is the distinction recognized in American society between the relationship of faith and the individual, faith and the community, and faith and the actual operation of government. In short, faith, properly understood, creates a spiritual, moral, and psychological foundation, which affects how the individual lives his life. In America, it is typically a moderating force in one's life, checking the excesses of the darker side of humanity, which in turn contributes to the civility of society. Even those who reject faith are not utterly devoid of its implications. For example, one has regular interactions with others whose faith affects or sways the nonbeliever's behavior, even without formally recognizing or accepting the faith itself. Moreover, society is imbued with the influences of faith. It is impossible to escape it. Therefore, even for those who do not consciously or formally embrace a faith, the teaching and practicing of faith create the moral and value-based belief system of so many others in society. This is an organic process, not theocratic or otherwise coercive.

It is possible to have, for example, a biblical or liturgical worldview, or a more formal or orthodox faith belief or perspective, and serve in the government without the desire, purpose, or conviction to impose that faith on others by governmental coercion—that is, negative power. This is well understood in America. And there are reasons for it.

For example, as previously noted, Christianity is the majority faith in America. But it is not the country's official or formal religion. In fact, Christianity does not preach political control over societies or administrative control over governments, unlike Islam, which I will elaborate on shortly. Thus, in America, the individual's pursuit of knowledge and science not only coexists with faith but springs from the influences of faith and are part of man's internal makeup.

Therefore, positive power originates not from mankind's hand or mind, although certainly its practical and earthly application does, but its origin is transcendent and inherent. When we speak of universal or eternal truths—the Golden Rule ("Do unto others as you would have them do unto you"), the Ten Commandments (e.g., "Thou shall not kill"), good and evil, etc.—these are fundamentally moral precepts understood and engrained in the human conscience and openly expressed in free and democratic societies. They are known to be true throughout the world, including among those who are oppressed by tyrannical governments and regimes, by the less educated or uneducated, by people of all faiths or no faith. This is not to say that all individuals, cultures, or regimes adhere to these eternal truths. Some are evil, power-hungry, irrational, etc. Man's existence is strewn with horrific examples of his cruelty, from ancient history to modern times. Of course, man's imperfection is both well known and well established. But *knowing* what is right from wrong, for instance, is distinct from *doing* what is right rather than wrong.

The examination and understanding, or at least the desire to understand what makes positive power (and its differentiation from negative power), do not end here. In addition to its references to natural law and the Creator, the Declaration of Independence drew from the knowledge of philosophers, among others, and their conception of society and mankind. For example, in a May 8, 1825, letter to Henry Lee, Thomas Jefferson, the original author of the Declaration, explains: "When forced . . . to resort to arms for redress, an appeal to the tribunal of the world was deemed proper for our justification. This was the object of the Declaration of Independence. Not to find out new principles, or new arguments, never before thought of, not merely to say things which had never been said before; but to place before mankind the common sense of the subject; . . . terms so plain and firm as to command their assent, and to justify ourselves in the independent stand we . . . compelled to take. Neither aiming at originality of principle or sentiment, nor yet copied from any particular and previous writing, it was intended to be an expression of the American mind, and to give to that expression the proper tone and spirit called for by the occasion. All its authority rests then on the harmonizing sentiments of the day, whether expressed, in conversations, in letters, printed essays or in the elementary books of public right, as Aristotle, Cicero, Locke, Sidney Etc."[4]

Importantly, America, like much of the West, was born from *the fusion of faith and enlightenment.* As such, while faith is distinct from government, the latter being the organization of law by and through man-made institutions, the fusion of which I speak *informed* the authors of America's Declaration and Constitution on the *prudent and humane order* of governmental affairs.

I understand that my beliefs and observations thus far in this chapter will not be shared by all, although they will be shared by many, if not most. My purpose is not to reach some kind of impossible consensus or to preach about religion or faith, since others are far more capable than I in that regard. Rather, I am sharing what I intuit and reason, what I have learned, observed, and experienced, to describe the essence of a just and humane society and its relationship to what I call positive power.

By contrast, for example, "political Islam"—as Dr. Zuhdi Jasser, a prominent Muslim scholar, founder of the American Islamic Forum for Democracy, and a leader in the Muslim reform movement, refers to it—seeks the centralized control over mind, body, society, and government. He explains that "Islam has yet to go through an enlightenment and reform against theocracy and for individual liberty and universal human rights. The dominant 'establishment' of the Muslim community in the West and abroad supports Islamism and its believers, the Islamists. . . . Like theocrats, Islamists and their sympathizers see faith as monolithic and do not tolerate diversity of interpretation."[5] Recounting his days in college, Jasser explains that Muslim campus groups promoted a form of Muslim identity that "wasn't about faith . . . [but] rather about their political agenda and especially their anti-Israel motives, their antisemitism, and was pretty much dominated by the Palestinian movement."

Jasser argues that the people of the Muslim faith deserve

much better than this. He notes that "the vast majority of Muslims are still a constituency that are not spoken for by anybody. . . . Hopefully, we can grow our bandwidth to do that."[6]

Tocqueville put it this way: "Mohommed professed to derive from Heaven, and he has inserted in the Koran, not only a body of religious doctrines, but political maxims, civil and criminal laws, and theories of science. The Gospel, on the contrary, only speaks of the general relationship of men to God and to each other—beyond which it inculcates and imposes no point of faith. . . ."[7] Indeed, in America today, Jasser notes that "Muslim Brotherhood legacy groups like Council on American-Islamic Relations (CAIR), Islamic Society of North America (ISNA), Islamic Circle of North America (ICNA), Muslim Students Association (MSA), and Muslim Public Affairs Council (MPAC) do not accept that devout Muslims exist who reject their ideas."[8]

In his book *A Battle for the Soul of Islam*, Jasser decries the preaching and writing of Sayyid Qutb, "one of the most prominent thought leaders of the Muslim Brotherhood and political Islam." Jasser explains that "[w]hile the roots of

Islamism can be traced back hundreds of years . . . with the ideas of 'pure' Islam," Qutb's 1964 book, *Milestones,* has significant influence even now.[9]

Qutb often mentions *jahilyyah,* which he defines as the state of ignorance of the guidance of God. What is extremely significant about this is that in Qutb's view the entire Western world was riddled with jahilyyah. At the same time he considered most Muslims of his time to be suffering from such ignorance . . . due to what he considered by watering down through the ages of "pure" Islam (in part because of Western influences but also due to what he considered Muslims tampering with the "purity" of Islam) so that it no longer existed.

Qutb saw it as his mission to revive such "pure" Islam, with its very strict interpretation of shariah law, and to never give an inch in terms of adopting or compromising with Western values, which he considered devoted to materialism, violence, and racism. . . .[10]

Finally, as Jasser notes, in his book Qutb writes:

> Our foremost objective is to change the practices
> of this society. Our aim is to change the jahili
> system at its very roots—this system which is
> fundamentally at variance with Islam and which,
> with the help of force and oppression, is keeping
> us from living the sort of life which is demanded
> by our Creator.
>
> Our first step will be to raise ourselves above the
> jahili society and all its causes and concepts. We
> will not change our own values and concepts either
> more or less to make a bargain with this jahili
> society. Never! We and it are on different roads,
> and if we take even one step in its company, we
> will lose our goal entirely and lose our way as well.[11]

Consequently, the constant bloody wars among different Muslim sects, including in Syria, Yemen, Lebanon, and
elsewhere, and the targeting of the West by a long list of Islamist organizations, such as Hamas, Islamic Jihad, and
al-Qaida, as well as Islamist states that support terrorism,
such as Iran, Qatar, and others, provide ample evidence of the

bloody Islamist impact both within individual countries and throughout the world, on Muslims and non-Muslims alike.

Furthermore, Western societies and governments do not seem to comprehend or wish to deceive themselves into ignoring, rationalizing, or excusing the dire peril Islamism represents, despite multiple acts of terrorism committed against them and threats of more and worse to come. In some cases, Western governments hope to avoid the consequences of Islamist ideology through appeasement, negotiation, or financial arrangements.

As of this writing, Iran—an Islamist dictatorship that has spread terrorism and murder throughout the Middle East and beyond, repeatedly demands the annihilation of the United States and the Jewish state of Israel (and has fired hundreds of missiles into Israel), has attempted to assassinate the president of the United States, has killed and maimed American soldiers and citizens, and has made alliance with the Communist Chinese government—is hell-bent on completing the development of nuclear weapons and intercontinental missile–delivery systems. Despite multiple agreements with the West and assurances that it has no intent on building nuclear weapons, the Islamist regime is about to have what is called a nuclear breakout—that is, nuclear weapons.

Iran has lied, cheated, and deceived multiple American

administrations, international organizations, European countries, etc., on its path to a nuclear breakout. Yet the United States and the West still hope to reach another deal to prevent Iran from crossing the finish line, and Iran will oblige them. As long as the Islamist regime survives, so too will its nuclear ambitions, despite any paper agreement or short respite.

There is no clearer example of the clash between negative and positive power—between a terrorist Islamist dictatorship and Western democracies, where the mind-sets, principles, and goals could not be more different. Indeed, in addition to what has already been said, deception, or in Arabic *taqiyya*, is believed to be a legitimate if not necessary strategy against non-Muslims.

Writing in the *Middle East Quarterly*, Raymond Ibrahim explains that "[a]ccording to Shari'a—the body of legal rulings that defines how a Muslim should behave in all circumstances—deception is not only permitted in certain situations but may be deemed obligatory in others." In his book *At-Taqiyya fi'l-Islam* (*Dissimulation in Islam*), Professor Sami Mukaram, a former Islamic studies professor at the American University in Beirut, writes: "Taqiyya is of fundamental importance in Islam. Practically every Islamic sect agrees to it and practices it. . . . We can go so far as to say that the practice of taqiyya is mainstream in Islam, and that those few sects not practicing it diverge from the mainstream. . . . Taqiyya is very prevalent in Islamic politics, especially in the modern era."[12]

"[I]n Islam," writes Ibrahim, ". . . war against the infidel is a perpetual affair—until, in the words of the Qur'an, 'all chaos ceases, and all religion belongs to God.' In his entry on jihad from the *Encyclopedia of Islam*, Emile Tyan states: 'The duty of the jihad exists as long as the universal domination of Islam has not been attained. . . .'" [Ibid.]

Among other things, this explains why Iran enters negotiations urged by the West and signs nonproliferation agreements it has no intention of complying with, as the West deludes itself and Iran lies and deceives its way to a nuclear breakout.

Again, to be clear, my focus is on Islamists, particularly among certain Muslim governmental and religious leaders, and their exercise of negative power, not Muslims per se.

Like Marxists, Islamists obviously reject liberty. However, Marxism rejects faith altogether and in fact insists on the eradication of not only faith but, like Islamists, all historical and social ties that contradict or compete with its ideology and delay or interfere with the inevitable revolution.

For Marxists, faith is said to be a fiction that shrouds the truth, dupes the people, and is incompatible with a new social and economic order. Faith is an illusion incompatible with reason. It denies man direct control of his own fate, provides a mystical escape for a soulless society, and sustains society's status quo and class structure.

Nonetheless, Marxism and Islamism share their disdain for the West and seek to destroy it. Hence, you see Marxists and Islamists openly working together against the West. In America they protest and riot as one on college campuses against the United States and Israel. In foreign policy, for example, Communist China and Iran have established a military and economic alliance. Prominent American Marxists in Congress, such as Senator Bernie Sanders, support the Islamists, and Islamists, such as Representative Rashida Tlaib, support the American Marxists. Both are typically members of the Democrat Party or mostly aligned with it.

Marx had nothing but dripping contempt for religion. In December 1843–January 1844, he famously wrote that religion is "the opium of the people":

Man makes religion, religion does not make man. Religion is, indeed, the self-consciousness and self-esteem of man who has either not yet won through to himself, or has already lost himself again. But man is no abstract being squatting outside the world. Man is the world of man—state, society. This state and this society produce religion, which is an inverted consciousness of the world, because they are an inverted world. Religion is the general theory of this world, its encyclopedic compendium, its logic in popular form, its spiritual point *d'honneur* [of honor], its enthusiasm, its moral sanction, its solemn complement, and its universal basis of consolation and justification. It is the fantastic realization of the human essence since the human essence has not acquired any true reality. The struggle against religion is, therefore, indirectly the struggle against that world whose spiritual aroma is religion.[13]

Marx adds that "[r]eligious suffering is, at one and the same time, the expression of real suffering and a protest against real suffering. Religion is the sigh of the oppressed creature, the heart of a heartless world, and the soul of soulless conditions. *It is the opium of the people.* The abolition of religion as the illusory happiness of the people is the demand for their real happiness. To call on them to give up their illusions about their condition is to call on them to give up a condition that requires illusions. The criticism of religion is, therefore, in embryo, the criticism of that vale of tears of which religion is the halo."[14] (Italics added.)

"Criticism has plucked the imaginary flowers on the chain not in order that man shall continue to bear that chain without fantasy or consolation," declares Marx, "but so that he shall throw off the chain and pluck the living flower. The criticism of religion disillusions man, so that he will think, act, and fashion his reality like a man who has discarded his illusions and regained his senses, so that he will move around himself as his own true Sun. Religion is only the illusory Sun which revolves around man as long as he does not revolve around himself."[15]

"Once man is freed from the shackles of faith," Marx argues, "the long string of deceit unravels, the slate is then clean, he sees clearly the injustices, corruption, and oppression of the society surrounding him. Thus, he can begin anew, understanding the true nature of things, and join in the revolution of the proletariat." As Marx states: "It is, therefore, the task of history, once the other-world of truth has vanished, to establish the truth of this world. It is the immediate task of philosophy, which is in the service of history, to unmask self-estrangement in its unholy forms once the holy form of human self-estrangement has been unmasked. Thus, the criticism of Heaven turns into the criticism of Earth, the criticism of religion into the criticism of law, and the criticism of theology into the criticism of politics."[16]

The overlay of Marxism with so-called modern-day progressivism (American Marxism) is unmistakable. Woodrow Wilson and his peers essentially plagiarized and customized large swaths of Marxist ideology and turned it into their own. Wilson's break from the Declaration of Independence and America's founding principles appears everywhere in his writings and speeches. Again, he insisted that concepts like eternal truths, natural law, unalienable rights, and so forth, and a focus on the individual and free will rather than the state, were quaint relics applicable only to the time in which they were asserted. They are neither relevant nor binding on the present or future, which are and will be in a constant state of movement manipulated and managed by masterminds.

One need not be theoretical about the disastrous human consequences resulting from the abandonment of positive power. Nothing focuses the mind better than the myriad real-life examples over the last century or so, and currently, of human genocide, mass incarceration, the obliteration of civil liberties, widespread poverty, etc., rooted in the negative power of Marxist ideology specifically and autocratic regimes generally. Although its Western progeny is of a different degree and manner, it is nonetheless a poison that finds opportunity in the fissures and rifts of any democracy, eating away at its bedrock and framework. This is the nature of the progressive movement.

In Marxism, unlike, for example, Islam, there is no fusion of faith with coercion in that there is no faith or higher order with which to fuse. Instead, Marxism replaces faith with a cultlike, man-made order where there is no higher order than man, or more precisely certain men. Indeed, even reason is whatever man says it is, or more specifically, whatever the ruling class says it is. Hence, both faith and reason are repudiated. There can be no conflict of ideas or interests, no compromise or settling. Conformity and uniformity of belief and behavior are essential to Marxists and Islamists, as well as other forms of autocratic enforcement. In point of fact, like Islamism, coercion is central to Marxism, as is the destruction of Western enlightenment and, necessarily, the advocates, tools, and institutions of positive power. The result is the collusion of Marxists and Islamists on America's college campuses demanding the eradication of Israel, America, and the West. And the alliances built by Communist China with Islamist regimes, such as Iran.

On the other hand, positive power nurtures that which Marxism, Islamism, and like entities seek to eradicate—the human spirit, virtue, self-consciousness, individual sovereignty and free will, unalienable rights, the competition of ideas, speech and debate, self-reliance, and other attributes of human interaction and innate character that contribute to a moral, vibrant, and healthy civil society.

In America today, like much of the West, most public debate about politics circles around who exercises power, almost to the exclusion of the meaning, purpose, and nature of power, which are central to understanding positive power. Although the "who" part of power is an essential area of inquiry and discussion, as I have explained at length in these chapters (e.g., separation of powers versus centralized coercion), it is not enough, as I have also described. The former, without more, is to debate the issue of power on the terms of negative power—that is, the abandonment of the quintessence of positive power and the civil society for a secular view of power unmoored from the principles that informed America's Founders and the Constitution's Framers. As I noted earlier, Mises observed that we are all philosophical Marxists now, whether we know it or not. Is this not the quandary faced today in America and throughout the West?

Of course, at times there are overlaps between positive and negative power, where the lines are not so clear or where one can be said to be a manifestation, in degrees, of the other. I alluded to this earlier in the book. In every democracy, soft negative power exists, which is more like positive power when in purpose and practice it improves the lot of the individual and society. No system, philosophy, or analysis of both is perfect or capable of perfection, not when dealing with the mind of mortal man. But neither time nor the confines of this book make chasing such exceptions possible or useful. For the purposes of this discussion, acknowledging what should be obvious is good enough.

4

ON LANGUAGE

There are endless treatises, ancient and new, on rhetoric and dialectic approaches to thought and communication. Rather than get into a long and largely esoteric inquiry and history of both (although I personally find it fascinating), it is more useful for the purposes of this book to evaluate language as it relates to the present-day applications of negative and positive power.

Language has many purposes, of course. But at its core, language is about communication. And there are many types of communication and many purposes for it as well. I will organize them into two basic categories: the power *of* language and the power *over* language. Again, this distinction has been discussed over the ages and in recent times in an infinite number of ways. That said, I shall use them here to make certain fundamental points, understanding that they are distinguishable in significant ways.

The pursuit and maintenance of negative power require the utilization of negative techniques of communication, including manipulation, deception, repetition, deceit, concealment, distraction, and fearmongering, in language that is intimidating, self-serving, and orchestrated. It is an approach that seeks to arouse prejudices and stifle independent thought. The purpose is to exert power *over* language and to control the population without moral reservations. Indeed, morality itself is said to be relative or nothing but an abstraction concealing the rot of open societies and democracies and obfuscating the exploitation of the people.

In the political context, when language is applied this way, it strikes a central part of the democratic system, denying the body politic information with which to make knowledgeable, qualitative, and collective decisions. Of course, this is the intention of its practitioners. Moreover, communication of this sort exists for the purpose of arousing and angering the citizenry and exhorting them to action that is destructive of the existing society and their own lives and lifestyles in service to the demagogue and his aims. Inasmuch as the people and their consent are the only legitimate and just source of government, the entire enterprise becomes corrupt and malevolent. Unfortunately, citizens acquiesce to it, regurgitate it, or even demand it (where applicable, vote for it), believing there is no other course or that it is the best course—until it is too late to reverse course without an abrupt and often violent revolt. But for many, suffering persists for an extended period of time.

For example, prior to the Russian Revolution, *Britannica* finds that in Vladimir Lenin's 1902 pamphlet, *What Is to Be Done*, he argues—quoting *Britannica* here—"that the propagandist, whose primary medium is print, explains the causes of social inequities such as unemployment or hunger, while the agitator, whose primary medium is speech, seizes on the emotional aspects of these issues to arouse his audience to indignation or action. Agitation is thus the use of political slogans and half-truths to exploit the grievances of the public and thereby to mold public opinion and mobilize public support. Propaganda, by contrast, is the reasoned use of historical and scientific arguments to indoctrinate the educated and so-called 'enlightened' members of society, such as party members."[1]

The combination of agitation with propaganda is, as *Britannica* further explains, agitprop. "The term *agitprop* originated as a shortened form of the Agitation and Propaganda Section of the Central Committee Secretariat of the Communist Party in the Soviet Union. This department of the Central Committee was established in the early 1920s and was responsible for determining the content of all official information, overseeing political education in schools, watching over all forms of mass communication, and mobilizing public support for party programs. . . ."[2]

Again, for Marxism and other forms of autocratic ideologies and governing systems, negative power is exercised through language that is tailored to lord over the people and control the society and culture. Language is a tool of the state that serves the state. It takes on an *official* character. It is limited, prescribed, and restricted. It compels certain types of speech and suppresses other forms (censorship). In essence, it is "organized propaganda,"[3] as the late Hannah Arendt, historian and philosopher, defined it. Simply put, it is thought control of the people.

Arendt explained further that what she called "totalitarian propaganda" involves "the use of indirect, veiled, and menacing hints" of violence to nonbelievers, claims of "scientific prophecy as distinguished from old-fashioned appeals to the past" and to "absolutist systems . . . which suppress men from this history of the human race."[4] It employs absurd "predictions . . . to avoid discussion" for "only the future can reveal its merits."[5] Moreover, Arendt observes that totalitarian propaganda highlights socialism and race as two key categories of exploitation because they neatly lend themselves to group identification and exploitation—that is, class and ethnic warfare.

It is not by mistake that class and ethnic warfare, among other forms of exploitation, are employed incessantly by American Marxists.

Consequently, the goal is to subvert the civil society and the principles, values, and beliefs on which it was established, corrupt the public spirit and civic harmony, and reject compromise and accommodation. The people must be unmoored from and cleansed of their history, faith, and family. Service to the totalitarian state and its utopian fiction is the highest calling, if not the only calling, and all other forms of experience and socialization are impediments and hindrances to "the cause."

Of course, democracies are not immune to this plight. In fact, they are susceptible to it. Negative power and, therefore, negative language exist in all societies, albeit to a different degree than in totalitarian regimes, and which I earlier referred to as soft negative power. However, an examination of its influence in democracies first requires a review of positive language in democracies.

Again, positive language emphasizes the power *to*, whereas negative language emphasizes the power *over*. Positive language taps into the individual and societal benefits of communication, including persuasion, interaction, truth-seeking, and the competition of ideas. It is language that is solicitous, factual, respectful, tolerant, informative, and well intentioned. The power of language is to reason and to think freely and, in the political realm, to encourage debate, inquiry, deliberation, contemplation, and learning. Thus, free speech is an essential value and precept in the application and exercise of positive power in an open society and democracy.

While free speech may and often does lead to societal consensus, its exact meaning is debated and disputed even now. It does not lend itself to an easy definition. It is better understood through a contextual description and elucidation by example. Nonetheless, it is a foundational and requisite principle in all healthy democracies and is clearly the counterweight to the forced uniformity of thought and beliefs, and conformity of behavior, sought and imposed by autocracies and authoritarian democracies.

In point of fact, consensus is how democracies function. Consensus is reached through the free will of individuals and their liberty of conscience, open interaction, and debate, not imposed by despots, governments, or political movements. It is power that works its way through the body politic and government from the bottom up, not the top down. Furthermore, it not only allows for but actually encourages the expression of minority or nonconformist views that, from time to time, can become the consensus view, with certain key exceptions I will discuss shortly.

There are also myriad kinds of speech most would consider foul, inciteful, threatening, etc., that are regulated or even banned. This is not the subject of this chapter or the context of this discussion. Nor are other forms of delineated speech, such as commercial speech, defamation, intellectual property, or criminal solicitation. Here, the focus is on power, and more specifically on unraveling the nature and character of positive and negative power.

That said, if a minority or nonconsensus view takes the form of, for example, agitprop, thereby inciting coercive action against the free speech of others through intimidation, threats, or violence, it ceases to be free speech or an exchange of ideas and an instrument of persuasion, but their opposite.

Thus, free speech in these circumstances, while remaining the free speech of the speaker, is used to destroy the free speech of others. As such, it is no longer positive language. It is negative language used in pursuit of negative power—that is, a weapon with which to pummel free speech.

For example, as recently witnessed on college campuses throughout America, such as Columbia University, trespassing, tent encampments, no-go zones, blockades, and vandalism—including taking over school buildings, graffiti on college property, and broken windows—are not protected free speech. Neither is shouting down counterprotesters with bullhorns and loudspeakers or spitting on, physically intimidating, threatening, and bullying Jewish students and faculty, forcing them to hide, lock themselves in rooms, and miss classes. Of course, these are the mob tactics of tyrants and totalitarians. This would be considered soft negative power bordering on, and promoting a higher level or intensity of, negative power. The ambition and motivation is to ramp up the degree and reach of power in such a way as to spark, for example, a Marxist-Islamist revolution against an open and democratic society.

Moreover, when these tactics are unleashed on behalf of foreign enemies, including a genocidal terrorist group like

Hamas, often funded and coordinated by them directly or indirectly through terrorist states like Qatar, and frequently, but not exclusively, at the coaxing or exhortation of foreign students and immigrants, and the stated purpose is a war on the West, including the usurpation of the civil society, the collapse of the democratic government, and the annihilation of a race of people—the Jewish people—there is obviously no relation or relevance to actual free speech. It is, as Lenin put it, agitprop, but in this instance not only in the hands of Marxists but Islamists as well. Again, this is where the liberty of the few, if it persists unabated, destroys the liberty of the many. In this case the intent is to wrest control from the people by and for the Marxist-Islamist agenda with intimidation, threats, and violence.

Moreover, the power-hungry must use negative language not only to forcibly advance their agenda but to conceal their faults and defects from the people to maintain their control. Positive speech is both a mainstay of open societies and democracies and a revealer of the defects of negative power. In the case of Marxism, Ludwig von Mises explains, "What really destroyed Marx was his idea of the progressive impoverishment of the workers. Marx didn't see that the most important characteristics of capitalism was the large-scale production for the needs of the masses; the main objective of capitalists is to produce for the broad masses. Nor did Marx see that under capitalism the customer is always right. In his capacity as a wage earner, the worker cannot determine what is to be made. But in his capacity as a customer, he is really the boss and tells his boss, the entrepreneur, what to do. His boss must obey the orders of the workers as they are members of the buying public. . . ."[6] In Marxist regimes, such as China, North Korea, Cuba, Venezuela, and Nicaragua, and other forms of authoritarian rule, torture, long prison sentences, or even death is meted out to the poor souls who would dare notice the horrendous conditions and circumstances, or talk about them, let alone challenge them. And there are typically domestic monitors and spies to ensure that they do not.

Additionally, two simple questions prove the lie of the Marxist workers' paradise. Who has a better life in nearly all respects? The assembly-line worker in America and the West, or the assembly-line worker in any Marxist or other form of autocratic regime? Of course, in America and the West. Indeed, where are the largest middle classes with the largest number of mostly free, mostly satisfied, and patriotic people? In America and the West, or in any Marxist or other form of autocratic regime? Of course, in America and the

West, which is why totalitarian regimes build walls to force their people to stay, whereas the United States builds walls to manage the influx of people escaping these regimes.*

For the tyrant, positive speech in the form of free speech is the gravest threat. He must build and maintain a cocoon of centralized control over society and culture. Negative language is among his greatest weapons for acquiring and maintaining power. And if the tyrant is to survive, he must institute constant purges and purifications of the population, spreading fear and terror throughout the population, for which language is weaponized.

Conversely, and to underscore the point, free speech is requisite to all other freedoms. It is also how individuals and societies learn, reform, improve, progress, etc. It is how governments are held to account or adjust to the will of the people. However, to assume its permanence, even where, as in America, free speech is enshrined in the First Amendment of the Constitution, would be a fatal conceit.

In America, as in much of the West, free speech is

---

* I hesitate to talk in terms of "class," since this is a Marxist invention, as nature does not create human economic classes and, in fact, Marx never actually defined what he meant by class. But for purposes of the book, it is a necessary and handy reference.

increasingly under assault. Not by the violent force of a foreign tyrant, although the threat is always there, but by the self-righteous demands of mostly factions and cabals within the country who find voice and empowerment in academia, the media, and the Democrat Party. They push various forms of negative power and, as such, coercion and ultimately authoritarianism. And, of course, in America the government insists it is done to protect the public from "mal-information, disinformation, and misinformation," among other things.

Among the most prominent of these pernicious present-day movements is *wokeism/cancel culture*, an intolerant and fanatical social and political crusade that demands thought and behavior control by banning words, giving words new meaning, creating new words, and tagging individuals, groups, and businesses with what is effectively a modern-day scarlet letter for noncompliance or what they perceive as insufficient obeyance. It employs intellectual suppression, silences dissent, and seeks to enforce ideological conformity through language and discourse control.

Unsurprisingly, wokeism/cancel culture is a product of the Frankfurt School's Critical Theory (a German-Marxist think tank of sorts), which I discuss at length in my book *American Marxism*. Briefly, it emphasizes and prioritizes dividing and categorizing people by race, sex, and gender as the basis of class struggle, without abandoning altogether strict economic classifications and struggles— what I have termed the Americanization of Marxism. But its techniques are similar: the deconstruction of existing traditions and institutions, vilifying dissenters, maligning history, and cloaking a destructive and extreme ideology in the language of social and political progress and rights. Nonbelievers and dissenters are to lose their jobs, occupations, and sources of income as an example to others who might defy the movement.

Wokeism/cancel culture adapts the same oppressor-oppressed formulation as traditional Marxism—that is, conflict theory. For example, if you are white and/or heterosexual and/or Christian, you are presumed to be an oppressor. For the movement, identity politics is the new and most crucial political and social class struggle of the day. The emphasis is not, for example, on the workers' paradise and the means of production, but on destroying and devouring the existing culture. The culture, it is argued, has been established by the equivalent of the bourgeoisie and is the source of inequality (now inequity), including economic dislocation, social injustice, etc.

Therefore, not only the government but, more importantly, the society must be "fundamentally transformed."

Another spin-off of Marxism is *postmodernism*. As explained by Dr. James Lindsay, founder of New Discourses, "it sees the construction of society through the way language is organized in complicated webs of meaning called 'discourses.' The postmodernists read a lot of power into discourses . . . and their theory is roughly the idea that the real source of Marx's 'superstructures' of society are constructed in language, discourses, and claims to knowledge. For them, knowledge is all socially constructed, and therefore truth claims—whether true or not—are all mere applications of the politics of those who happen to hold power at that particular time and place in human history."[7]*

Clearly, then, language, whether negative or positive, is like power itself, mutable. Depending on the user's intentions, it can be liberating, coercive, transformative, informative, manipulative, persuasive, uniting, disuniting, transparent, ambiguous, emotional, conversational, etc. It has as many characteristics as human beings themselves. It reflects human nature and conveys the mental processes of the human mind. Thus, language

---

* This theory is not altogether different from what Wilson and the early progressives preached.

control is mind or thought control—negative language. Free speech, properly understood, is mind- or thought-liberating—positive language. It can be said, therefore, that language is behind power, and power is behind language. It influences power, reveals power, and reflects power.

Another feature of negative power is that it seeks to dominate the society, culture, and body politic. Our Constitution is constructed against domination by any person, party, faction, mob, or despot. In addition to the core principle of separation of powers, discussed earlier, the language of the Constitution is fashioned toward the same ends. The three governing branches are assigned not only overarching areas of authority—legislative, executive, and judicial—but also relatively detailed responsibilities within those authorities. The language determines the grant and distribution of governing power. Hence, the importance of applying the actual text of the Constitution and the intent of its authors when interpreting and applying it.

There is a great risk when altering our Constitution, or any constitution built on the foundation of positive power (with soft negative power limitations, again, intended to secure and promote positive power), that more damage may be done than improvement. It is one thing to make governing changes within the Constitution—for example, the number of judicial districts established, the arrangement of congressional districts—but it is altogether different to make changes to the Constitution's design. Article V provides two intentionally cumbersome methods for amendment.

> Congress, whenever two thirds of both Houses
> shall deem it necessary, shall propose Amendments
> to this Constitution, or, on the Application of the
> Legislatures of two thirds of the several States, shall
> call a Convention for proposing Amendments.
> The proposed amendments shall be valid to all
> intents and purposes, as part of this Constitution,
> when ratified by the Legislatures of three fourths
> of the several States, or by Conventions in three
> fourths thereof. . . .[8]

These amendment processes require and ensure the support from a large majority of the citizenry for their federal and state representatives to alter the nation's governing document.[9] This is how it should be. No officials, temporarily elected or even appointed for life (federal judges), should have or do have the power to radically and fundamentally alter a democracy without the broad consent of the governed. Such a decision is a societal one, not the decision of a centralized ruling class or, worse yet, a single committee, tribunal, or official. Of course, the Constitution has required modification on occasion and has been amended. I have proposed amendments to the Constitution in my book *The Liberty Amendments*, through the convention-of-states process. This is fundamentally different than amending—that is, rewriting—the Constitution through extraconstitutional and, therefore, *un*constitutional means.

Indeed, in America, as in Israel and other Western nations, such a nefarious and potentially ruinous circumstance exists. For example, when judges perfidiously and illegitimately seize for themselves the power to make law, rather than honestly interpret or apply it, their actions are ruinous. As they are often the final word on matters of constitutional and legal outcomes, their manipulation of those words is diabolical. The governing foundation of the country and the constitutional arrangement are severely undermined and weakened. Public support for our institutions is shaken. The law becomes unstable and unpredictable. Nonetheless, the interpretation and application of the law become binding edicts, although the law itself has been bastardized. The judges are rulers, not honest referees. And these edicts, being the final word, have so corrupted the system that lawful recourse is mostly a dead end. This leads not only to societal disunity and distrust but the unraveling of the civil society and the possible incitement of a dangerous and even violent reaction over time.

As of this writing, the Trump administration has been faced with scores of federal lower-court judges, most of whom were selected by former Democrat Party presidents, who are carefully cherry-picked by litigants who are also officials of the Democrat Party or who are of a political and ideological bent shared by the party, issuing rulings that plainly violate the Constitution's separation of powers as these judges arrogate to themselves authority granted to the president and the executive branch. They are substituting their personal and political policy preferences for those of the president and wrapping them in constitutional and legal jargon.

In short, they are constitutionalizing and legalizing their own agendas and giving them the imprimatur of legitimate authority.

Scores of lawsuits have been brought, resulting in dozens of restraining orders, injunctions, and outright reversals of presidential decisions about executive branch ministerial actions.[10] These court edicts have disrupted all manner of presidential judgments and determinations, including the hiring and firing of federal employees, the content of department websites, access to federal payroll information and other data, the restructuring of federal departments, the deportation of illegal-alien gang members and criminals, the elimination of government-wide woke policies, withholding taxpayer funds from foreign governments or related organizations, eliminating funding for transgender procedures for children, military readiness decisions including banning transgender individuals from military service, ending the housing of biological men in prison cells with biological women, etc. Thus, the unitary executive, under a president elected nationwide by the citizenry, is being molested in many important respects by a phalanx of lawyers turned judicial oligarchs who have seized power for themselves.

Charles Schumer, the Senate Democrat Party leader, was also the leader of the Senate prior to January 2025, when Joe Biden was still president. On March 19, 2025, on the PBS program *News Hour*, Schumer openly and publicly declared that he and the Senate Democrats installed hundreds of ideological partisans/activists to lifetime federal judicial positions to thwart President Trump should he be elected:

Our democracy is at risk because Donald Trump shows that he wishes to violate the laws in many,

many different ways. The good news here is we did put 235 judges, progressive judges, judges not under the control of Trump last year, on the bench, and they are ruling against Trump time after time after time. And we hope that the appellate courts, when it gets up there and the Supreme Court will uphold those rulings. They restored the money to NIH. . . . [W]e're in over one hundred lawsuits against them, and we are having a good deal of success. It's only at the lower court level right now. . . .[11]

As explained in Chapter 1, this is precisely as Montesquieu warned:

[T]here [is not] liberty if the power of judging is not separate from the legislative power and from the executive power. If it were joined to legislative power, the power over the life and liberty of the citizens would be arbitrary, for the judge would be the legislator. If it were joined to executive power, the judge could have the force of an oppressor. All would be lost if the same man or the same body of principal men, either of nobles, or of the people, exercised these three powers: that of making the laws, that of executing public resolutions, and that of judging the crimes or the disputes of individuals.[12]

Appeals have been made to various appellate courts and the Supreme Court to undo much of the damage that has been done by the lower federal courts. So far the results have been mixed. That said, the bigger issue is the precedent this sets if it is not soon reversed, given the aggressiveness of the underlying judicial tyranny and the likely enshrinement of this illegitimate exercise of power when (not if) the higher courts are populated with a majority of like-minded judicial oligarchs.

The late constitutional scholar Raoul Berger made a crucial and highly relevant point in his book *Government by Judiciary* about a proposal at the Constitutional Convention that would have granted the judiciary the power it now claims—which was overwhelmingly rejected by the delegates. He explains:

Despite the fact that the proposal [for a council of revision of the national judiciary that should

examine every act of Congress and by its dissent
constitute a veto] had the support of [James]
Madison . . . it was rejected for reasons that
unmistakenly spell out the exclusion of the
judiciary from even a share in policymaking.[13]

But Woodrow Wilson's view has prevailed, fundamentally altering separation of powers and the power of the judiciary, which is why the Trump administration has been swamped with third-party litigation and unfavorable lower-court *policy* decisions. This is the judicial tyranny that Wilson and his progressive contemporaries envisioned.

Remember, Wilson argued for the power of unelected judges and bureaucratic administrators, operating outside the limiting parameters of the Constitution and without the interference of the voters, remaking society at the direction of masterminds, experts, and other presumed elites who share the American Marxist ideology. He specifically rejected the ideas of John Locke, whose influence on the American revolutionaries was enormous, and Montesquieu, whose influence on the Constitution's Framers was central to their thinking and approach to governance.

Wilson's viewpoints, which are prevalent in the

Democrat Party and beyond and held by their judges, were inspired by, among others, German philosophers Georg Wilhelm Friedrich Hegel and later Karl Marx—the former idealized the state and its dialectic evolution, resulting ultimately in a fascist-like state;* the latter applied dialectic analysis to materialism to justify the proletarian revolution.[14] Again, to emphasize the point, the Democrat Party today is the party of progressivism/American Marxism, the ideology of which is antithetical to America's founding principles.

There is little wonder, therefore, that the Trump administration has been subjected to an unprecedented onslaught of judicial interventions and obstructions, ultimately intended to violate the Constitution's separation of powers and in defense of the administrative state built over the course of the last century. As such, there is a clash between the tyrannical exercise of negative power by the judiciary, an unelected and unrepresentative body, and the constitutional exercise of positive power by the president, who is chosen by the citizenry in a nationwide election. Both use positive language to describe their own actions and negative language to

---

* *Dialectic* is generally understood to mean a method of examining opposing ideas until the ultimate truth reveals itself.

characterize each other. However, the two cannot be fundamentally and simultaneously right, and are not.

The courts and their ideological and political patrons are using agitprop—that is, propaganda and activism clothed as law and justice. Agitprop is not limited to autocratic governments exercising negative power, nor is it limited to street activism. Here, the courts are using it as part of a political movement in the manner of Marxist quasi-politburos. This is further evidence of authoritarian democracy.

***

An additional area worthy of examination involves *truth*. By truth I do not mean in a relative sense—that is, what one might honestly and wrongly believe to be the truth, etc. Rather, the intentional use of positive language to communicate what is widely known and commonly understood to be truthful by the person or government using it, in contrast to the intentional use of deceit, slander, and falsehoods in a form or way to suggest, imply, or flat-out portray it as truth. This is similar to other forms of negative language, such as propaganda and manipulation, that may be used in an identical manner. They may also contain a kernel of truth. However, truth is a real thing, and the inexactitude with which it may or may not apply in a certain situation or form of communication does not negate its existence. For example, eternal truths are, in fact, universally known whether or not they are adhered to and embraced.

Let us look at another constitution, this time the Soviet Constitution of 1936, a.k.a. the Stalin Constitution, specifically parts of Chapter X, on the Fundamental Rights and Duties of Citizens, that crystallize the point:[15]

> **ARTICLE 123.** Equality of rights of citizens of the USSR, irrespective of their nationality or race, in all spheres of economic, state, cultural, social and political life, is an indefeasible law.
>
> Any direct or indirect restriction of the rights of, or, conversely, any establishment of direct or indirect privileges for, citizens on account of their race or nationality, as well as any advocacy of racial or national exclusiveness or hatred and contempt, is punishable by law.
>
> **ARTICLE 124.** In order to ensure to citizens freedom of conscience, the church in the USSR is separated from the state, and the school from the church. Freedom of religious worship and freedom

of anti-religious propaganda is recognized for
all citizens.

ARTICLE 125. In conformity with the interests
of the working people, and in order to strengthen
the socialist system, the citizens of the USSR are
guaranteed by law:

a) freedom of speech;

b) freedom of the press;

c) freedom of assembly, including the holding of
mass meetings;

d) freedom of street processions and
demonstrations; these civil rights are ensured by
placing at the disposal of the working people and
their organizations printing presses, stocks of paper,
public buildings, the streets, communications
facilities and other material requisites for the
exercise of these rights.

ARTICLE 126. In conformity with the interests
of the working people, and in order to develop
the organizational initiative and political
activity of the masses of the people, citizens

of the USSR are ensured the right to unite in public organizations—trade unions, cooperative associations, youth organizations, sport and defense organizations, cultural, technical and scientific societies; and the most active and politically most conscious citizens in the ranks of the working class and other sections of the working people unite in the Communist Party of the Soviet Union (Bolsheviks), which is the vanguard of the working people in their struggle to strengthen and develop the socialist system and is the leading core of all organizations of the working people, both public and state.

ARTICLE 127. Citizens of the USSR are guaranteed inviolability of the person. No person may be placed under arrest except by decision of a court or with the sanction of a procurator.

ARTICLE 128. The inviolability of the homes of citizens and privacy of correspondence are protected by law.

In its civil liberties language, Chapter X of the Stalin Constitution is modeled after major parts of our Constitution's

Bill of Rights. But it goes much further, adding language that claims to ensure extensive economic benefits and security as human rights. Yet we all know that Stalin's Soviet Union was one of the most horrific, genocidal Communist regimes of all. Indeed, it was among the most monstrous autocracies of any kind ever. Thus, the language in these articles, and the articles taken together, which promise a free and open society where the government recognizes and protects individual human rights and liberties and provides for the economic and welfare rights of the citizens, are loathsome lies. Here, positive language is used as an atrocious deception to advance the gravest form of negative power—mass imprisonments and executions. It has absolutely no connection to the truth. Stalin did not believe a word of this.

In his book *Stalin's Genocides*, Hoover Institution senior fellow Norman Naimark, a history professor at Stanford, argues that "the Soviet elimination of a social class, the kulaks (higher-income farmers), the subsequent killer famine among Ukrainian peasants, and the notorious 1937 order that called for the mass execution and exile of 'socially harmful elements' as 'enemies of the people' were, in fact, genocide. 'I make the argument that these matters shouldn't be seen as discrete episodes, but seen together,' says Naimark, an authority on the

Soviet regime. 'It's a horrific case of genocide—the purposeful elimination of all or part of a social group, a political group.' Stalin had nearly a million of his own citizens executed, beginning in the 1930s. Millions more fell victim to forced labor, deportation, famine, massacres, and detention and interrogation by Stalin's henchmen. 'In some cases, a quota was established for the number to be executed, the number to be arrested,' says Naimark. 'Some officials overfulfilled as a way of showing their exuberance.'"[16]

Why would such a diabolical despot establish such a constitution? Sometimes, if not often, belief in a false idea is enough to make it seem true, at least in the minds of those among the citizenry who want to believe, including those who self-identify as patriots of their country and are loyal to it. This is an *illusory truth*. Moreover, the country and government are often seen as one in the same—as a whole. To disbelieve in the government is to disbelieve in the country. Thus, Stalin's constitution was the motherland's constitution—Russia's constitution—despite being a pack of lies. It is worth noting that the supposed civil liberties in the constitution did not apply to either the police or the Ministry of the Interior, the monitoring and enforcement arms of the Soviet police state.

The language in Stalin's Constitution is intended to deceive the people inside and outside the country and, perversely, justify the regime's domestic terror tactics, which were carried out in the name of the people and the cause.

Marx said there would be a period of despotism to eliminate all opposition to the proletariat and sanitize all aspects of society from the past before the workers' paradise would come into being. The brutality of the state is for the good of the people and undertaken in their name. However, as experience demonstrates, the period of despotism disappears only if the regime falls. *Truth is the enemy of the state* and those who control it.

Mao Zedong's barbarous Communist regime was marked by relentless mass murders totaling tens of millions of dead. From 1966 to 1976 alone, during the so-called Cultural Revolution, the "mass killings . . . consisted of five types: 1) mass terror or mass dictatorship encouraged by the government—victims were humiliated and then killed by mobs or forced to commit suicide on streets or other public places; 2) direct killing of unarmed civilians by armed forces; 3) pogroms against traditional 'class enemies' by government-led perpetrators such as local security officers and militias; 4) killings as part of political witch-hunts (a huge number of suspects of alleged conspiratorial groups were tortured to death during investigations); and 5) summary execution of captives, that is, disarmed prisoners from factional armed conflicts. The most frequent forms of massacres were the first four types, which were all state-sponsored killings. The degree of brutality in the mass killings of the Cultural Revolution was very high. Usually, the victims perished only after first being humiliated, struggled and then imprisoned for a long period of time."[17]

President Xi Jinping, the current Communist Party leader of China, has been ruling the country for a decade now and clearly sees himself as Mao's progeny. The Hudson Institute explains that "[t]he party's grip on power is premised on denying 1.4 billion people their human rights. Over the past decade, the CCP [Chinese Communist Party] has committed genocide and crimes against humanity against Uyghur Muslims, dismantled freedom and human rights in Hong Kong, Macau, and Southern Mongolia, sought to erase Tibet's culture and language, persecuted Christians, cracked down on freedom of religion or belief for people of all faith traditions, and targeted human rights defenders and dissidents. The CCP increasingly commits abuses beyond its borders and undermines international human rights by actively undermining sovereignty in myriad ways, including through transnational repression."[18]

The numerous examples of mass murder and repression in Marxist regimes over the decades, although widely condemned in Western countries, do not seem to deter the appeal of Marxist theories, doctrines, or language in the West. Excuses are made for the terrible "excesses" of Marxist genocidal rulers, but, we are told, Marx himself and his doctrinal writings, in one form or another, are more relevant than ever, require some adjustment, are misunderstood, etc. The articles and books are so numerous that it is impossible to cite them here. Moreover, university courses are not merely about Marxism but promote it, and professors who preach it are also legion.

The vast amount of propaganda about and for Marxism throughout Western culture, including in the United States, is prodigious—despite the monstrous inhumanity it has unleashed. Hence, the amount of time I have spent in this book—which is, after all, about power—on the subject.

***

Of course, truth is often abused in democratic societies as well. To be clear, it is different in kind and degree than in autocratic regimes, but the danger it poses in a democracy is not to be ignored or downplayed.

In relation to politics and government, candidates, public officials, the media, etc., the people are routinely the target of deceit intended to convince them of a viewpoint, to vote for them or someone they support, champion a policy or cause, etc., by employing negative language, including fabrications, misrepresentations, and exaggerations. For example, Senator Bernie Sanders, a Marxist[19] who self-identifies as a Democratic Socialist, has repeatedly accused the Republican Party of supporting tax cuts for billionaires and of being the party of billionaires—a typical Marxist-based class-warfare mantra. Of course, three of the Democrat Party's most notable supporters are among the wealthiest men in the world, each multibillionaires—George Soros, Bill Gates, and Warren Buffett. The Republicans are not without billionaire supporters, of course, most notably Elon Musk, a former Democrat Party supporter. But it is Sanders, among others, and the Democrat Party who consistently use this line of attack on the Republicans. Yet of the over 77 million people who voted for Donald Trump for president and the hundreds of thousands who contributed to his campaign as well as the campaigns of other Republican candidates, the percentage who were billionaires is so small as to be incalculable. A party or candidate that is "for billionaires" could never achieve such an electoral landslide. And the tax cuts proposed and instituted, whether President John F. Kennedy's proposed tax cuts, which were adopted a few months after his assassination, in 1964,[20] Ronald Reagan's tax cuts in 1981,[21] or Donald Trump's first- and second-term tax cuts, lowered income tax rates for all taxpayers, if not outright eliminating taxes for certain lower- and middle-income citizens. They also provided improved tax conditions for businesses to help spur economic growth and job creation. This is not a partisan observation but a matter of fact and record. But Marxist class warfare, even of the older sort that stresses the bourgeois–proletariat economic divide, remains a potent propaganda tool of the modern Democrat Party.

Additionally, when Representative Alexandria Ocasio-Cortez, who also self-identifies as a Democratic Socialist, denounces the Republican Party and President Trump as wanting to destroy Social Security and Medicare, it is another falsehood intended to incite fear and anger. I can think of no Republican president or Republican Congress that has sought to destroy either program. Why would they? In fact, President Trump has repeatedly and publicly stated he will not touch either program. Other Republicans have, over the years, proposed reforms to both programs to help ensure their future viability, in response to the trustees who issue annual reports warning of their prospective insolvency. And each time the proposed reforms are met with Democrat Party charges of Republicans "wanting to destroy" the programs. Hence, the saying that Social Security and Medicare are the "third rail" of politics—that is, do not touch them or even talk about adjusting them. The allegations against the Republicans are even more irrational, given that millions of Republicans receive benefits from Social Security and Medicare and many of them vote. Why would Republicans run on an agenda of destroying these programs when to do so would disunite their party and ensure electoral defeat? Obviously, they would not. But the purpose of the negative language is not to communicate the truth. It is to deceive, manipulate, and upset the public in the pursuit of votes and power.

However, unlike autocracies, in an open democratic society, positive language can be employed to rebut, disprove, and discredit what is said or written, as I have done here—in this case, about the Republican Party and taxes, Social Security, and Medicare. Again, this is an indispensable value of free speech.

As just alluded to, a favorite negative language technique

is *repetition*. With repetition, the more likely you are to accept and believe the supposed truth of what is being repeated, even if it is untruthful. Moreover, the more you see or hear something, the more likely you are to remember it.

Numerous psychologists call it the *mere exposure effect*. According to Charlotte Nickerson, "The mere exposure effect is a cognitive bias where individuals show a preference for things they're more familiar with. Repeated exposure to a stimulus increases liking and familiarity, even without conscious recognition. Essentially, the more we encounter something, the more we tend to prefer it, based on familiarity alone."[22] Of course, there are exceptions to the rule, but the rule itself holds. And it can be used as a particularly sinister and infectious propaganda device in the hands of demagogues and tyrants. I refer to this as *negative repetition*.

Repetition as such destroys the conscious mind, the ability to reason, and moral clarity. Yet it is the autocrat who claims that only through reason and its scientific application can a truly just, equal, and prosperous society be born and the fullness of the individual realized through the collective of the state. Of course, employing negative language to secure and exercise negative power destroys man's nature, no matter how many philosophers, past and present, insist otherwise. Is this not the dictator's way? Is that not the purpose—to control, force, and compel conformity, obedience, and groupthink?

People are thought to be too ignorant, obtuse, emotional, self-absorbed, etc., to reason for themselves. But that is precisely what the dictator squeezes out of them—the ability to reason, think, and act independent of the state.

Repetition often involves sloganeering as propaganda—that is, the use of simple, easy-to-recall labels, catchphrases, mental images, mottos, jingles, sayings, and so forth. They can be more immediate, effective, and long-lasting in their impact and mental footprint. For example, "tax cuts for the rich," "warmongers and neocons." Repetition can also take the form of symbols, salutes, emblems, signs, songs, and the like.

However, not all repetition is the same. It can actually be used in service to positive power, hence *positive repetition*. Let us begin with the basics. For example, athletes and dancers repeatedly practice the same movements. Singers memorize lyrics, and students memorize historical facts and mathematical formulas. This demonstrates that repetition, when applied in a positive way and for the right purposes, enhances learning, improves the mind, and creates success.

In the military, among other institutions, repetition ensures discipline, routine, and order, all necessary to build an effective fighting force. The old saying "Practice makes perfect" certainly is apt in these instances.

That which distinguishes negative and positive repetition is the *purpose* of the repetition—that is, for what purpose is the mind being rewired? The next question is, what *behavior* is being discouraged or encouraged?

In America, classes from kindergarten through twelfth grade would start each morning with the Pledge of Allegiance. "I pledge allegiance to the Flag of the United States of America and to the Republic for which it stands, one nation, under God, indivisible, with liberty and justice for all." The purpose was to build allegiance and unity for the country (patriotism), its vital principles of freedom and goodness (eternal truths), and acknowledge—as in the Declaration of Independence— the role of providence (God) in American society. The behavior that was encouraged was to be an upright American citizen. Unfortunately, many school districts have dropped the Pledge from their daily routine. Some have dropped the reference to God to not offend objecting secularists and non-believers, thereby forsaking a fundamental attribute of the American experiment, as discussed in Chapters 2 and 3.

Positive repetition, which is intended to build allegiance to and patriotism for the country, is reinforced behavior that is crucial to the survival of a democracy. It does not, and is not intended to, serve as one part of a multipart mind-controlling regimen of dictated and directed orthodoxy, as in authoritarian regimes. It is an affirmation of values and beliefs that reinforce an open and free society. This also explains opposition to the Pledge and its reference to God, among other displays of allegiance to the country, by American Marxists and their ilk, who seek to displace the existing society with their own political and social construct.

There are infinite ways to analyze language, which means there needs to be a cutoff point for this book. For me it will be the language of the modern revolutionaries, the power-hungry, the malcontents, and others who wish for the existing societies in the West to crumble in the pursuit of some imagined utopia or paradise. By this I do not mean what has already been discussed, but the larger imperative—that is, the forced journey on which, for example, the American Marxists wish to drag us.

It is no accident that the ideologies of tyranny present themselves as otherworldly, inevitable, and futuristic through *positive language* that creates images of an ideal. Moreover,

Marx and others portray their fictional worlds as ending in a perfect state of nirvana, despite the fact that no mortal construct can create a final state of man, let alone nirvana. Indeed, Marxism provides the indisputable evidence of this fact. Nonetheless, its pursuit, even in America, requires a troubling level of subjugation of the individual to the ideology and power of the state.

In *Rediscovering Americanism (and the Tyranny of Progressivism)*, I explain:

> Obviously, as one would expect, there is not
> a seamless symmetry among and between the
> various American progressives and certain of the
> principal philosophers who influenced them.
> However, there certainly are significant similarities
> of outlook and attitude toward mankind,
> economics, law, politics, and government;
> there is a zealous belief and commitment in
> reengineering both man's nature and his social
> environment toward egalitarian and utopian
> ends; and there is an affinity for centralized rule,
> whether of fascistic or socialistic kind, some

hybrid thereof, or some derivative thereof. For these reasons and others, the American progressive philosophers, intellectuals, and politicians uniformly disparaged the principles of the American founding, the American civil society, and the American constitutional system. Whether idealistic historicism, material historicism, historic dialecticism, material dialecticism, synthesizing of opposites, actualizing individualism, conscious individualism, egalitarianism, the social sciences, the behavioral sciences, etc., the individual is swept up into, and ultimately disfigured by, a whirlwind of ideological concepts and impossibilities. As the oppressiveness and impracticability of progressivism spread, the more hardline and belligerent become its proponents and enforcers. Ultimately, it leads to the unraveling of the civil society.[23]

Of course, the power of these ideological movements knows no bounds and is not limited by a nation's sovereignty or geographic borders. Most were born in Europe. Today, the

West is inundated with manifestos and the language of tyranny—negative language—flowing through the culture and society. Not enough is being done to challenge and confront it, which is one of the purposes of this book.

By now it should be apparent that the subject of power is complex and complicated, making it difficult if not impossible to easily break down into wholly separate and distinct subclassifications. There is an overlap between and among its various and numerous parts, such as positive and negative language. Nonetheless, there is no other way to analyze and unravel the subject than to at least chew on it. Despite its defects and imperfections, it is hugely useful and important to do so.

5

ON RIGHTS

In this chapter, I begin with the premise, underscored by the Declaration of Independence, that individual and human rights, liberty, and equality predate governments because they do not originate from governments.

> We hold these truths to be self-evident, that all
> men are created equal, that they are endowed by
> their Creator with certain unalienable Rights,
> that among these are Life, Liberty and the pursuit
> of Happiness.—That to secure these rights,
> Governments are instituted among Men, deriving
> their just powers from the consent of the governed.[1]

The significance and magnitude of these two straightforward and concise sentences are impossible to overstate. Rights, or moral truths, are God-given through natural law and, therefore, are transcendent and universal. Through right reason, man discovers these truths or is innately aware of them.

Thomas Jefferson, who authored the original draft of the Declaration, was certainly not alone in this view. It was the collective belief of the Founders, including George Mason (the primary author of the Virginia Declaration of Rights), Benjamin Franklin (the primary author of the Pennsylvania Declaration of Rights), John Adams and Samuel Adams (the primary authors of the Massachusetts Declaration of Rights), and others.

Section 1 of the Virginia Declaration of Rights, which predates the Declaration of Independence by a few weeks (June 12, 1776), states:

> That all men are by nature equally free and
> independent and have certain inherent rights,
> of which, when they enter into a state of society,
> they cannot, by any compact, deprive or divest
> their posterity; namely, the enjoyment of life
> and liberty, with the means of acquiring and
> possessing property, and pursuing and obtaining
> happiness and safety.[2]

As noted earlier, however, the 19th-century philosophers who inform the Democrat Party, its progressive/American Marxist ideologues, and their Western counterparts are, among others, Hegel and Marx. Of course, Woodrow Wilson's influence as a scholar and president was enormous. Their views were contemptuous of the foundational principles relied on in the Declaration and the consensus view of the Founders.

Clearly, the basis for America's founding and the ideology of the American Marxist are utterly incompatible. Indeed, this is at the heart of the competition for governing power or, more accurately, the power struggle that exists today and has for one hundred years or more—that is, two opposite and irreconcilable worldviews about the individual and humanity itself competing for power.

There is no liberty without rights, and rights precede government. However, the societal effectuation and earthly manifestation of those rights are determined by power—negative or positive power. Out of societies nations are established—some imposed, some with the consent of the people, some more spontaneous than others, some more gradual than others, some civil, some primitive, etc. Not all societies establish governments, but all societies establish a hierarchy in one form or another and in one way or another. In the civil society, the purpose is to secure and protect both the unalienable rights of each individual and those of the community of individuals who voluntarily come together for that purpose. Just laws are adopted by the consent of the people, meaning a majority of the society's members, but the majority is to represent the best interests of the entire society.

Although the civil society is distinct from government, the government is to reflect the purposes and character of the civil society. It is to safeguard it and, again, the unalienable rights of the individual in society. In *Federalist* No. 51, James Madison explains, in part:

> A dependence on the people is, no doubt,
> the primary control on the government; but
> experience has taught mankind the necessity of
> auxiliary precautions. This policy of supplying,
> by opposite and rival interests, the defect of
> better motives, might be traced through the
> whole system of human affairs, private as well
> as public. We see it particularly displayed in all
> the subordinate distributions of power, where the
> constant aim is to divide and arrange the several

offices in such a manner as that each may be a check on the other that the private interest of every individual may be a sentinel over the public rights. These inventions of prudence cannot be less requisite in the distribution of the supreme powers of the State.[3]

Here, Madison is arguing in support for the proposed Constitution's division of powers. The influence of Locke and Montesquieu is obvious. I have previously written extensively about America's founding, including the beliefs and arguments of key philosophers and statesmen, in my book *Rediscovering Americanism (and the Tyranny of Progressivism).*[4] Thus, the purpose of this chapter is not to regurgitate what has already been said but provide a concise basis for discussing the nature of rights, the relationship between power and rights, and the ensuing power struggle to retain those rights.

For me, however, Madison was among the most significant and essential statesmen involved in the birth of the United States, due to his role in America's founding and governmental structure as "the father of the Constitution," and his positions in government, including as the fourth president of the United States. Therefore, I return to his writings to further inform us on the understanding he and his fellow patriots had of rights.

On March 29, 1792, Madison penned an iconic essay on *rights* and *power* in the context of *property rights*. I choose to provide the essay without edits to ensure that I do not diminish its understanding, impact, and importance. It is fairly concise yet thorough.

> This term in its particular application means "that dominion which one man claims and exercises over the external things of the world, in exclusion of every other individual."
>
> In its larger and juster meaning, it embraces every thing to which a man may attach a value and have a right; and *which leaves to everyone else the like advantage.*
>
> In the former sense, a man's land, or merchandize, or money is called his property.
>
> In the latter sense, a man has a property in his opinions and the free communication of them.
>
> He has a property of peculiar value in his religious opinions, and in the profession and practice dictated by them.

He has a property very dear to him in the safety and liberty of his person.

He has an equal property in the free use of his faculties and free choice of the objects on which to employ them.

In a word, as a man is said to have a right to his property, he may be equally said to have a property in his rights.

Where an excess of power prevails, property of no sort is duly respected. No man is safe in his opinions, his person, his faculties, or his possessions.

Where there is an excess of liberty, the effect is the same, tho' from an opposite cause.

Government is instituted to protect property of every sort; as well that which lies in the various rights of individuals, as that which the term particularly expresses. This being the end of government, that alone is a *just* government, which *impartially* secures to every man, whatever is his *own*.

According to this standard of merit, the praise of affording a just securing to property, should be sparingly bestowed on a government which, however scrupulously guarding the possessions of individuals, does not protect them in the enjoyment and communication of their opinions, in which they have an equal, and in the estimation of some, a more valuable property.

More sparingly should this praise be allowed to a government, where a man's religious rights are violated by penalties, or fettered by tests, or taxed by a hierarchy. Conscience is the most sacred of all property; other property depending in part on positive law, the exercise of that, being a natural and unalienable right. To guard a man's house as his castle, to pay public and enforce private debts with the most exact faith, can give no title to invade a man's conscience which is more sacred than his castle, or to withhold from it that debt of protection, for which the public faith is pledged, by the very nature and original conditions of the social pact.

That is not a just government, nor is property secure under it, where the property which a man has in his personal safety and personal liberty,

is violated by arbitrary seizures of one class of
citizens for the service of the rest. A magistrate
issuing his warrants to a press gang, would be
in his proper functions in Turkey or Indostan,
under appellations proverbial of the most
complete despotism.

That is not a just government, nor is property
secure under it, where arbitrary restrictions,
exemptions, and monopolies deny to part of
its citizens that free use of their faculties, and
free choice of their occupations, which not only
constitute their property in the general sense of
the word; but are the means of acquiring property
strictly so called. What must be the spirit of
legislation where a manufacturer of linen cloth is
forbidden to bury his own child in a linen shroud,
in order to favor his neighbor who manufactures
woolen cloth; where the manufacturer and
wearer of woolen cloth are again forbidden the
economical use of buttons of that material,
in favor of the manufacturer of buttons of
other materials!

A just security to property is not afforded by

that government, under which unequal taxes oppress one species of property and reward another species: where arbitrary taxes invade the domestic sanctuaries of the rich, and excessive taxes grind the faces of the poor; where the keenness and competitions of want are deemed an insufficient spur to labor, and taxes are again applied, by an unfeeling policy, as another spur; in violation of that sacred property, which Heaven, in decreeing man to earn his bread by the sweat of his brow, kindly reserved to him, in the small repose that could be spared from the supply of his necessities.

If there be a government then which prides itself in maintaining the inviolability of property; which provides that none shall be taken *directly* even for public use without indemnification to the owner, and yet *directly* violates the property which individuals have in their opinions, their religion, their persons, and their faculties; nay more, which *indirectly* violates their property, in their actual possessions, in the labor that acquires their daily subsistence, and in the hallowed remnant of time which ought to relieve their fatigues and soothe their cares, the influence have been anticipated, that such a government is not a pattern for the United States.

If the United States mean to obtain or deserve the full praise due to wise and just governments, they will equally respect the rights of property, and the property in rights: they will rival the government that most sacredly guards the former; and by repelling its example in violating the latter, will make themselves a pattern to that and all other governments.[5]

Thus, sovereignty is in the individual and the people, not the government. Again, as mentioned earlier in the book, God is the sovereign, whose sovereignty is reflected in his children—we, the people. No government is legitimate but for the consent of the people. Therefore, representative government is imperative. It checks the rulers and serves the people through elections. Limited government is the only kind of government that can reflect and respond to the will of the people. Massive bureaucracies with hundreds of departments and agencies populated by millions of employees making and issuing regulations (laws) without input from the people conflicts with representative government and functions without the consent of the people. Importantly, people outside the government are to be represented by people inside the government. How is this possible under these circumstances? As I asserted earlier, the government today is increasingly devouring the private sector—that is, the civil society, becoming a power unto itself.

Here is the key: The Founders and Framers believed and understood that *governments are formed to protect our natural rights*. Hillsdale College president Dr. Larry Arnn explains that "[e]ach individual is born with unalienable rights. Individuals come together to form peoples [a civil society], and each people has a natural standing to a separate and equal station. No man may be governed except by his consent. No people may be governed except by its consent."[6]

Therefore, positive power is the outgrowth of natural rights, as I explain in Chapter 2, and in America that positive power is incorporated within the Constitution. The connection between the Declaration and the Constitution is incontrovertible.

Consequently, when *members of the ruling class* besmirch and degrade the Constitution they swore to uphold, for their own aggrandizement or ideological designs, they are, in fact, intent on diminishing if not eradicating the rights of the people and their consensual role in the government—that is, the entire purpose of America's founding.

Again, there is no escaping that this is the project mostly of the Democrat Party, their media surrogates, and like-minded ideologues in academia and entertainment. Let me emphasize the Framers themselves understood that the Constitution might need adjustment on occasion. And in Article V they provided the two processes for amending it. The amendment processes, as noted earlier, intentionally involve the entire body politic and require its consent. They also require supermajorities to adopt proposed amendments. This is a far cry from members of the ruling class, whether judges, legislators, or presidents, altering the Constitution by assertion or, more likely, by manipulation, deceit, or stealth, and shrouding it in constitutional and legal language or concealing it within the haze of bureaucratic red tape. This is a mutinous encroachment on the rights of the individual, the civil society, and the Constitution that was intended to secure and protect them.

I again turn to Marxism, which, despite its various versions, provides the greatest, albeit not exclusive, threat to the American experiment. In fact, Marx directly and often denounced natural law and individual liberty, as all would-be autocrats must. For example, in *The Communist Manifesto*, Marx stated, in part:

> The selfish misconceptions that induce you
> to transform into eternal laws of nature and
> of reason, the social forms springing from
> your present mode of production and form
> of property—historical relations that rise and
> disappear in the progress of production—the
> misconception you share with every ruling class
> that has preceded you. What you see clearly in
> the case of ancient property, what you admit in
> the case of feudal property, you are of course
> forbidden to admit in the case of your own
> bourgeois form of property.[7]

By now this should be familiar, not only because of the earlier discussion of Marxism, but the earlier highlights from Woodrow Wilson's writings, where he condemned the Declaration as antiquated and the Constitution as both antiquated and a barrier to modernity and progress.

For Marx and his progeny, the idea of individual rights

is the problem. It is, he argues, intended to keep individuals as islands unto themselves, disconnected and isolated from each other. Each jealously guards his own interests, including property, and sees others as adversaries and antagonists, rather than as part of a society or a social being. This produces a dehumanized and hollow man. Remarkable, considering what we know about Marxism's unspeakable inhumanity.

For the broader society, Marx contends that capitalism produces neither liberty nor equality but rather inequality and self-centeredness. To be truly liberated, the individual must go through not only a political transformation but a social revolution—that is, cutting all social bonds to religion and even family, destroying the existing society, and remaking human beings—everything they have been taught, experienced, and think. After all, he alleges, the bourgeoisie control all aspects and nature of the political and social arrangements that spring from capitalism. Therefore, every bit of it must be eradicated.

Again from *The Communist Manifesto*, Marx writes:

Abolition of the family! Even the most
radical flare up at this infamous proposal of
the Communists.

On what foundation is the present family, the bourgeois family, based? On capital, on private gain. In its completely developed form, this family exists only among the bourgeoisie. But this state of things finds its complement in the practical absence of the family among the proletarians, and in public prostitution.

The bourgeois family will vanish as a matter of course when its complement vanishes, and both will vanish with the vanishing of capital.

Do you charge us with wanting to stop the exploitation of children by their parents? To this crime we plead guilty.

But, you say, we destroy the most hallowed of relations, when we replace home education by social.

And your education! Is not that also social, and determined by the social conditions under which you educate, by the intervention direct or indirect, of society, by means of schools, &c.? The Communists have not invented the intervention of society in education; they do but seek to alter the character of that intervention,

and to rescue education from the influence of
the ruling class.

The bourgeois claptrap about the family
and education, about the hallowed co-relation
of parents and child, becomes all the more
disgusting, the more, by the action of Modern
Industry, all the family ties among the
proletarians are torn asunder, and their children
transformed into simple articles of commerce and
instruments of labor.[8]

The power to destroy not just a government but the
deep and broad roots of an entire society—faith, values,
beliefs, family, friendships, other relationships, professions,
etc., and extinguish the knowledge, learning, lifestyles,
habits, and ties between fellow human beings and of human
existence—predictably requires not just a revolution, but a
horrifically violent social and societal convulsion followed
by unending and unbounded acts of genocidal and psy-
chotic tyranny, which eventually consumes itself. Hence,
my discussion earlier about the Soviet Union and China.
Indeed, not a single Marxist regime has ever or will ever
shake off its despotism or despots for the supposed final

stage of societal development. As Friedrich Engels put it, the state withers away:

> The interference of the state power in social relations becomes superfluous in one sphere after another, and then ceases of itself. The government of persons is replaced by the administration of things and the direction of the processes of production. The state is not "abolished," it withers away.[9]

The Marxist utopian state, and most other autocratic utopian states or states of utopia promised by power-hungry masterminds and revolutionaries, is, if you think about it, complete nonsense. Marx's writings, along with his partner Engels, are dripping with arrogance and anger, as well as absolute certainty and pomposity. Even a cursory examination of Marxism's application in one country and society after another proves it to be nothing more than an elaborate maze of absurdities and distortions about humanity, the impossibility of which has resulted in the misery and death of tens of millions.

Stanford University professor Robert A. Berman explains

that "Marxism was never about achieving an egalitarian so-ciety. It was about the pursuit of raw power." [10] "While for others, politics represents a realm of compromise and negotiation, for Marx, it was really the pursuit of power and the obligation to command. He described the state simply as 'the executive committee of the bourgeoisie,' meaning that politics was secondary to the economy. Moreover, he promised to abolish the state, and therefore politics, once Communism would eliminate class differences—so the story went, as the ultimate outcome of Communism would be a libertarian utopia of statelessness." [11]

Berman explains that "[n]othing, however, would be further from the truth. In practice, what Communism provided for was the development of a *nomenklatura*, a new class elite which talked the egalitarian talk while claiming for itself the privilege of dictators. The Communist cadre always knew better than the unenlightened populace, and therefore the cadre would claim the power to impose their views and programs on the rest of society. The real political legacy of Marxism was not the abolition of the state but, on the contrary, the expansion of the state over society, and the elevation of a Marxist elite over the populace." [12]

Given all we know about Marxism in particular, and

autocracies generally, and the imposition of negative power to destroy individual and societal rights and liberties, it is deeply distressing that for so many, including Democrat Party politicians and officials, broad aspects of Marxism are more prominent if not central in their mind-set than Americanism and the essential principles of our country's founding. To understand this contemporary reality is to comprehend the nature and worsening divide in our country, and the profound political and social disputes in which we find ourselves. For the ruling class, and its hunger for power, the American way is not satisfactory or fulfilling. The entire construct of individual sovereignty, unalienable individual rights, natural law, etc., and a government that is limited, divided, and representative restrains and suppresses powers that the ruling class craves. The negative power of Marxism is the polar opposite of the positive power of republicanism.

For the American Marxist, the source of rights is mankind. And not mankind writ large, but a faction of men who seize power in the name of impossible fantasies and mental inventions. Thus, the struggle is over who defines and assigns rights. Ultimately, and despite theories and ideologies to the contrary, they conclude that the power over rights, and hence the power over the individual and society, rests in who controls government. Therefore, in modern parlance, the endgame is not social justice, environmental justice, economic justice, equity, etc., but raw power. The rest is nothing more than propaganda in pursuit of that power. Is that not the true end of all autocratic regimes? *Power!* It is certainly true of Marx's view of rights. Any power from which individual rights and liberties are said to flow is an illegitimate power—that is, nothing more than a bourgeois contrivance and device. Therefore, the society and all that underlies and sustains it must be abolished.

For the American Marxist, the means is the relentless war on the nation's founding and Founders, American history, the Constitution and the law, freedom of speech, the family, the culture, faith, the economic system (capitalism), and more. It is a real and focused whole-of-society counterrevolution. Therefore, it is essential that they secure power inside or as the ruling class, where they plot to hold governmental power as long as they can and pass it to succeeding generations of like-minded ideologues.

They are unwilling to abrogate their power at the whimsy of the voter, even when and if they go through the motions of surrendering elective office to a victor outside the ruling class. Hence, the overarching importance of an omnipresent administrative state and an unelected judiciary to protect it—it being the permanent government. They are, at first, agencies of resistance, usurpation, and sabotage against the existing society, but eventually, as the power of the American Marxist proliferates and effectuates, it moves from the revolutionary phase to the coercion phase, increasingly taking on the characteristics of a police state.

Again, the consent of the governed and representative government via elections becomes more illusion than reality, and honored and legitimized only if the governed consent to the will of the ruling class. Indeed, their "for the people, the working class" language, as well as their class warfare and justice-seeking declarations, as explained in Chapter 4, are intended to deceive and manipulate. The instincts of the American Marxists are authoritarian. Their followers, like the rest of the people, are treated as dupes, with negative language, including righteous-sounding but self-serving propaganda.

To control the government is to control the distribution and enforcement (or nonenforcement) of rights—*not* God-given unalienable rights, of course, but so-called economic and social rights, which are the only rights that are said to matter, at least at first. The government must define these rights, since the individual or the people are considered incapable of it through their own actions and associations. The government can assign and deny economic rights and otherwise exploit and wield them—in the name of the greater cause. Those who object (to the denial of individual and economic rights) or otherwise stand in the way must be made to conform or face public and societal ridicule or worse. This supposed progress is, of course, inevitable, or leastwise must appear so. Shangri-la is always said to be within reach—if only the ruling class has more power and the individual less.

The extent to which not only Woodrow Wilson but later Franklin Roosevelt, the most revered and celebrated Democrat Party president and leader, borrowed from the Hegelian and Marxist concept of rights is indisputable. Indeed, on January 11, 1944, Roosevelt issued his Second Bill of Rights. As you read it, compare it to Stalin's 1936 constitution, discussed earlier, and the economic similarities will be obvious.

This Republic had its beginning, and grew to its
present strength, under the protection of certain
inalienable political rights—among them the
right of free speech, free press, free worship, trial

by jury, freedom from unreasonable searches and seizures. They were our rights to life and liberty.

As our nation has grown in size and stature, however—as our industrial economy expanded—*these political rights proved inadequate to assure us equality in the pursuit of happiness.*

We have come to a clear realization of the fact that *true individual freedom cannot exist without economic security and independence.* "Necessitous men [definition: "Necessitous men, are not, truly speaking, free men; but, to answer a present emergency, will submit to any terms that the crafty may impose on them."] are not free men." People who are hungry and out of a job are the stuff of which dictatorships are made. In our day these economic truths have become accepted as self-evident.

We have accepted, so to speak, a second Bill of Rights under which a *new basis of security and prosperity can be established for all*—regardless of station, race, or creed.

Among these are:

The right to a useful and remunerative job

in the industries or shops or farms or mines of
the nation;

The right to earn enough to provide adequate
food and clothing and recreation;

The right of every farmer to raise and sell his
products at a return which will give him and his
family a decent living;

The right of every businessman, large and
small, to trade in an atmosphere of freedom
from unfair competition and domination by
monopolies at home or abroad;

The right of every family to a decent home;

The right to adequate medical care and the
opportunity to achieve and enjoy good health;

The right to adequate protection from the
economic fears of old age, sickness, accident,
and unemployment;

The right to a good education.

All of these rights spell security. And after this
war is won we must be prepared to move forward,
in the implementation of these rights, to new goals
of human happiness and well-being. America's
own rightful place in the world depends in large

part upon how fully these and similar rights have been carried into practice for our citizens.[13]

In fact, virtually all references these days to civil liberties and civil rights are not about rights as understood by the Founders (e.g., in the Declaration and Madison's essay on property) but as defined by Marx. Wokeism and cancel culture destroy individual rights and the rights of the people in service to relatively small factions of people. The purpose is to, among other things, destroy the nuclear family, the parent–child social relationship, free speech, and independent thought, etc. This will be discussed further in the following chapter. That said, FDR's Second Bill of Rights, as it applies to economic and social rights, is simply echoing Stalin's constitution. Both Stalin and FDR appropriated from Marx his application of rights to economic socialism. (Of course, I am not arguing FDR was in any respect genocidal and despotic like Stalin. American Marxism is uniquely American, which is why I coined the phrase and wrote a book addressing it at length.)

Thus, the struggle between the Founders' understanding of rights and the Marx-FDR–Democrat Party understanding of rights will determine what kind of nation we will be—

a constitutional republic or an authoritarian democracy (or even a more aggressive type of autocratic society as time goes on). As I mentioned in Chapter 1, the longer-term trajectory of democracies is not encouraging. However, I also caution that trajectories are not to be confused with actual outcomes in a given situation or, here, in a given country. In America, we, the people, remain virtuous and resilient; also, not only do we reject revolution, we are deeply patriotic. However, the revolution waged by the American Marxists is not sudden and violent, but mostly gradual, surreptitious, and wrapped in deceit, making effective opposition more daunting. That said, I am even less sanguine about the chances of certain countries in Europe.

Some have argued that it is possible for social and economic rights to exist without some form of tyranny. The problem with this view is that the negative power associated with these supposed rights of necessity diminishes individual rights and, in fact, dismisses rights as they were understood by the Founders. Moreover, if there are constitutional and legal barriers creating parameters for social and economic rights, what are they? Power shifts from the individual to the government. There is simply no doubt about it. Therefore, to say there are limits—for example, by arguing that the rights as understood by the Founders work in unison or parallel with social and economic rights—is not to identify them in any concrete way. Instead, at best, there is a temporary overlap, which creates the barriers to tyranny, and the ambiguous social and economic rights proclaimed by their advocates, because the truth is that Marx was right when he said socialism is the last stage before Communism.

If there is to be a huge shift away from positive power for a so-called Second Bill of Rights, there should be an explicit understanding of what it means and where it is headed. To say, as another example, that the last century saw this huge movement toward a massive welfare state, including entitlements and such, and the American people have accepted it, and that these are the new rights that are now implicit in the Constitution, leaves a great deal unsaid and obscured about the future of governmental power. It enables the advocates of economic and social rights to create virtually any kind of painting they wish—impressionist, post-impressionist, but mostly abstract.

When it is said that there need not be a socialist revolution associated with social and economic rights, that assertion is a half-truth—that is, while the government need not own the means of production, for example, it must regulate it. And as the regulations prove insufficient, as they cannot achieve the kind of economic and social equality (now termed equity) promised or expected—which are extravagant and impossible—the answer will not be to abandon negative power for positive power associated with individual and societal rights and liberty, but to tighten the reins of control and centralization. In fact, the targeted beneficiaries and the true believers will become agitated and dissatisfied and demand more from the ruling class when their hopes and expectations are unmet. In short, government grows stronger and bigger, not less so, at the expense of the individual and society.

When looking further into the struggle over rights, and most crucially which rights approach will prevail, we see that there is a constant struggle to *be* the ruling class, a constant struggle *within* the ruling class, and a constant struggle *between the people and the ruling class*. Again, it is positive power and the rights approach of the Founders that provide civil lanes for compromise, tolerance, moderation, and peaceful resolution both in society and government. Negative power and the economic and social rights approach provide no such lanes and in fact weaken those that exist. To say that the people are satisfied and supportive of the massive welfare state, a welfare state that is not static and in fact history shows is always growing and consuming, is to say nothing about the accompanying centralization and coerciveness of government. The role of the people continuously diminishes, including their ability to defend their individual and societal rights. To the extent such lanes do exist, it is because of what remains of rights from the founding period.

The advocates of constitutionalizing economic and social rights, without the benefit first of a fulsome societal discussion followed by the wide-eyed participation of the body politic in either of the actual constitutional amendment processes, claim for themselves an open field on which to run. Both participatory democracy and representative republicanism, the hybrids and hallmarks of our constitutional system, are to be avoided and have been. The only question to be asked, according to the proponents, is the after-the-fact inquiry of whether people like and want to keep their benefits. Without more, presumably most people like to receive benefits, having become used to them if not reliant on them. Does this not prove the point? That is, what are the parameters for such an approach? What are the limits on government? The Constitution, they say in reply, as they usurp and breach it in pursuit of their Second Bill of Rights. But their approach is authoritarian in character. Consequently, they insist that this form of rights and the further empowerment of centralized and coercive government is *virtuous*. If challenged, they defend the use of negative power as, ironically, confined by positive power, the very power they are diminishing. Moreover, they rhetorically insist that if you disagree you obviously oppose helping the poor, the sick, and the underprivileged. Nor do you care about countless other societal maladies raised by the economic and social rights movements, including environmental, racial, economic, and so forth. The justifications for a pervasive central government with vigorous police powers are unlimited.

Therefore, for the American Marxist, authoritarian democracy is a virtue, for that is where they would eventually drag us. The broad and relentless application of negative power in the name of the downtrodden is said to be a righteous calling and endeavor. However, I am not the first to say (Aristotle, Cicero, Locke, Montesquieu, Benjamin Franklin, John Adams, C. S. Lewis, among innumerable others), nor will I be the last, that there is no freedom without virtue, but there are also endless examples of acts of oppression and inhumanity done in the name of virtue (e.g., Marx's workers' paradise). It is another one of those words, like democracy, used by republicans and tyrants alike, as discussed in Chapter 4.

It does not seem to occur to these individuals—or it

does, but they would rather not address it—that apart from the usual authoritarian characteristics of too much centralized power, a ruling class is not uniquely qualified, or well qualified at all, to manage society—that is, millions of individuals with diverse interests and backgrounds, collectively involved in billions of activities and interactions every single day. Despite all the written and spoken pablum about experts, professionals, educated elites, and so forth, equipped with the magic of reason (not to be confused with right reason, by the way), science (political and behavioral science, not the hard sciences), and all the rest—wisely, prudentially, and altruistically serving the greater good of society and the best interests of the people—we know from our own experiences as individuals and as a citizenry that no such ruling class exists. In point of fact, we know that incompetence and corruption are widespread, and practical experience and common sense are in short supply.

A major reason for the ruling class's noxious and unhinged hostility toward Elon Musk and the Department of Government Efficiency, or DOGE, is the fact that they did more in a few months' time to expose the vast and immense financial, programmatic, and policy disasters of the ruling class than at any time in the last century. They uncovered billions of dollars in waste, fraud, and abuse, subsidies for fringe and perverse events, antiquated computer and accounting systems, payments going to deceased and nonexistent people, the employment of far more people than necessary, money squandered overseas, and much more.

The institutionalized bloat and corruption have a large constituency not only within the ruling class but among its beneficiaries outside the regime. Unsurprising, it also has a political home in the Democrat Party, a public voice in the media, and defenders in academia. After all, they are the architects of the administrative state, going back in earnest to at least Woodrow Wilson.

This perfectly illustrates the corruption of the ruling class and the ideological and doctrinal irrationality and unattainability of American Marxism's agenda. There is no corner of the administrative state that is untouched by their influence. It is endemic, for it is the nature of such governments. Therefore, those who persist in promoting and defending the existing administrative state, without reining it in, limiting it, and controlling it, as well as the ruling class that gives it unfettered latitude and license, cannot be said to be of good and moral intentions. They are knowing and active facilitators of its immensity and all that naturally flows from it. The corruption of a power-hungry ruling class has infected them.

What does this have to do with rights? A great deal. Here, the ruling class and the administrative state, which in the best of circumstances and conditions pose life-altering and numerous threats to the existence of representative government, are knowingly and significantly unscrupulous. Thus, government is perverting the law, in America's case the highest governing law, the Constitution, and turning it into a weapon in service to itself and, consequently, against the civil society and the rights of the individual and the people. As Frédéric Bastiat explained:

> [W]hen [the law] has exceeded its proper function,
> it has not done so merely in some inconsequential
> and debatable matters. The law has gone further
> than this; it has acted in direct opposition to its
> own purpose. The law has been used to destroy its
> own objective: It has been applied to annihilating
> the justice that it was supposed to maintain;
> to limiting and destroying rights which its real
> purpose was to respect. The law has placed the
> collective force at the disposal of the unscrupulous

who wish, without risk, to exploit the person, liberty and property of others. It has converted plunder into a right, in order to protect plunder. And it has converted lawful defense into a crime, in order to punish lawful defense. . . .[14]

Clearly, it is impossible to discuss power and rights without the constant elucidation of Americanism and Marxism and contrasting the two. It is the progenies of Marx, and the entrails of his ideological activism, that blight the West and America today. There is no better time and place in this book, when much has already been explained and a proper intellectual foundation has been laid, to make clear that whatever one thinks of Marxism, and I think absolutely nothing favorable about it, Marx's theories and calls for revolution were written at a time when most of the world's economies were agrarian. Although there had been what is described as the First Industrial Revolution, which began around 1790, much of American capitalism was in its infancy. It was not until what is referred to as the Second Industrial Revolution, which began around 1870, that American capitalism exploded onto the scene, resulting in unimagined economic development, growth, and prosperity.

Although there is neither the room on these pages nor the time in this book to veer into the infinite ways in which open societies with largely market-oriented economic systems, and with governments that are both representative and limited in authority, overwhelmingly produce moral, humane, and just outcomes throughout the civil society—the propaganda and self-loathing of the American Marxist, the Democrat Party, academia, and the media aside—a powerful but concise reminder is compelled.[15]

The Second Industrial Revolution created extraordinary capital and wealth *and* a huge and, yes, comfortable middle class. And where and when our society wanes or fails, as all imperfect people and societies do, whether in economics or civil rights, etc., Americans have both the capacity and motivation to correct course. That is what positive power is about, and America's founding teaches us that. It is how a civil society not only survives but improves, reforms, and hopefully thrives. Of course, the same cannot be said of Marxist or other autocratic societies and regimes. Marx died in 1883, late enough to see the early stage of America's bursting industrial might. Nonetheless, the vast majority of what he wrote and argued had already been recorded in his books and essays. In fact, his most widely read paper, which he coauthored with Engels, was

The Communist Manifesto, which was penned in 1848, well before the early days of the Second Industrial Revolution.

My point is, putting aside all my other critiques of Marx, that his ideology was misplaced from the start. Capitalism, as he coined market economics, was (and is) a tremendous human and societal success not only for individuals but for the bulk of the people. The Second Industrial Revolution created technologies that changed the world forever, benefiting humankind from then until now. Indeed, so ubiquitous is the miracle of capitalism, swirling around us every day, its presence is mostly ignored and taken for granted. Instead, what we are taught in most schools and hear from the media and academia, as well as Democrat Party officialdom and American Marxists, is a relentless bombardment of propaganda and agitprop about class warfare, social injustice, and terminal inequity—all intended to poison the public mind and destroy the American experiment. The few short paragraphs that follow prove the entire Marx-materialism doctrine wrong.

Economist George Reisman, in his 1996 book, *Capitalism*, makes an overwhelming case for the universal benefits of capitalism—that is, its incredible material benefits for the individual and the people, which have absolutely nothing to do with class struggle. He explains that there is no class struggle at all.

Industrial civilization has radically increased life expectancy:

> In the twentieth century, in the United States, it
> has increased life expectancy from about forty-
> six years in 1900 for the present seventy-five
> years. The enormous combination of industrial
> civilization to human life is further illustrated
> by the fact that the average newborn American
> child has a greater chance of living to the age
> of sixty-five than the average newborn children
> of a nonindustrial society has of living to the
> age of five. The marvelous results have come
> about because of an ever-increasing supply of
> food, clothing, shelter, medical care, and all
> the conveniences of life, and the progressive
> reduction in human fatigue and exhaustion. All
> of this has taken place on a foundation of [actual]
> science, technology, and capitalism, which have
> made possible the continuous development and

introduction of new and improved products and more efficient methods of production. . . .

Famine has been ended, because industrial civilization has produced the greatest abundance and variety of food in the history of the world, and has created the storage and transportation systems required to bring it to everyone. This same industrial civilization has produced the greatest abundance of clothing and shoes, and of housing, in the history of the world. And while some people in the industrialized countries may be hungry and homeless . . . it is certain that no one in the industrialized countries needs to be hungry or homeless. Industrial civilization has also produced the iron and steel pipe, the chemical purification and pumping systems, and the boilers, that enable everyone to have instant access to safe drinking water, hot or cold, every minute of the day. It has produced the sewage systems and the automobiles that have removed filth from human and animal waste from the streets of cities and towns. It has produced vaccines, anesthesia, antibiotics, and all the other "wonder drugs" of modern times, along with all kinds of new and improved diagnostic and surgical equipment. It is such accomplishments in the foundation of public health and in medicine, along with improved nutrition, clothing, and shelter, that have put an end to plagues and radically reduced the incident of almost every type of disease.

As a result of industrialized civilizations, not only do billions more people survive, but in the advanced countries they do so on a level far exceeding that of kings and emperors in all previous ages—on a level that just a few generations ago would have been regarded as possible only in a world of science fiction. With a turn of a key, the push of a pedal, and the touch of a steering wheel, they drive along highways in wonderous machines at sixty miles an hour. With the flick of a switch, they light a room in the middle of darkness. With the touch of a button, they watch events take place ten thousand miles away. With the touch of a few other buttons, they talk to other people across town or across the world. They even fly through the air at six hundred miles per hour, forty thousand feet up, watching movies and sipping martinis in air-conditioned comfort as they do so. In the United States, most people can have all this, and spacious homes or apartments, carpeted and fully furnished, with indoor plumbing, central heating, air conditioning, refrigerators, freezers, and gas and electric stoves, and also personal libraries of hundreds of books, records . . . ; they can have all this, as well as long life and good health—as a result of working forty hours a week.[16]

Indeed, in the United States, a walk through a neighborhood supermarket (itself a word unheard-of less than a century ago) makes available to anyone and everyone more abundance and choices of food, beverages, over-the-counter pharmaceutical products, cleaning products, and toiletries, among other things, from every corner of the country and the planet, packaged to ensure their freshness and safety, than at any time in human existence. An assembly-line worker, plumber, electrician, bus driver, and janitor have more material goods at their fingertips today than Caesar, King George III, and Stalin ever did or could have imagined.

The real-world evidence and experience with the principles that underlay our Declaration of Independence are not mystical or theoretical or out-of-date or unproven or what have you. The human condition and rights that they articulate and establish are real, tangible, and contextual. They are on display and in play every minute of the day.

Conversely, the entire Marxist project is, as I said earlier, an evil fiction. It is the greatest deception, in the name of the people (the proletariat) and equality, ever produced. It plays into the jealousies man has, one for the other, by focusing on unequal economic outcomes. Of course, there can never be perfect equality, and therefore any and every imperfection, no matter how insignificant, is an occasion for Marxist exploitation and confirmation.

Marx also institutionalizes finger-pointing—that is, who is responsible for the individual's dissatisfaction and unhappiness. Marx does not recognize the individual and free will. Thus, the state and its (economic) system, and those who are said to have created it, sustain it, and benefit from it (the bourgeoise), are responsible for a person's difficulties and life challenges. Again, this is among the reasons Marx rejects individualism and free will, and relentlessly attacks the existing society (natural law and eternal rights), the state (representative democracy), the economic system (capitalism), and successful citizens (the bourgeoise) by smearing and demeaning them. They must be obliterated, every part of them, if the workers' paradise is to be achieved. Yet the society that comes closest to a workers' paradise is the American system.

Unfortunately, what I have described is an enormously effective psychological appeal (or should I say ploy) for several reasons. For starters, relieving a person of responsibility for his own failings, dissatisfactions, and unhappiness, and providing ready-made excuses is hugely comforting to that individual. The same thinking applies to individuals grouped into various categories—economic, racial, gender, age, geographic, etc. For Marx, it also lays the groundwork for the individual to surrender his rights and liberty for what he is told is the promised land. A better life, where everyone is said to be equal, where the workers are in control, and competition and conflict are replaced with sameness and single-mindedness—first as defined by the revolutionaries, and, once in control of the government, by the state.

For autocracies, and especially Marxism, redefining rights, assigning and denying rights, and applying rights to policy agendas and ideological aims is about controlling the dialogue about rights, actually controlling rights, and the quest for power.

In contrast, what is certain is that the preeminence of positive power, which in America sprouts from our Providence and founding principles, created a society in which the individual and the people are acknowledged as the true sovereign, and they can aspire to do great things that improve their own lives and those of others. This human progress is built within the context of a constitution, which institutes the kind of representative, divided, and limited government that has as its purpose to support and protect the founding principles.

If it sounds like I am a cheerleader for the American founding, I am. Not because of jingoism, but from observation and experience. Observation of the long history of mankind up to today, and experience as one living in the American society. Indeed, this is why I write books as I do, including this one, and ceaselessly warn of the vulnerabilities, threats, and dangers facing modern America.

As Thomas Paine declared in 1776 in his pamphlet *Common Sense*, "The cause of America is in a great measure the cause of all mankind."[17] He was right. The cause was and is universal.

6

ON LIBERTY

I have discussed liberty throughout the earlier chapters of the book but not in a sufficiently focused way. Indeed, liberty overlays any discussion about power and rights as it is connected to both. That said, I begin this chapter with the confession that no amount of writing about liberty can ever be adequate. The best I or, frankly, anyone else can do, or has done through the ages, is to give it our best shot. Nonetheless, some have done much better than others, and some have been downright mendacious and deceitful, even going so far as to define or use liberty to describe and promote its opposite—including Jean-Jacques Rousseau, Georg Wilhelm Friedrich Hegel, Karl Marx, and numerous others, past and present. This is the essence of negative language in support of negative power.

I begin by dismissing the ideas or premises that have taken hold in far too many places that liberty is found in the state or that true individual liberty (and fulfillment) is manifested in the collective or that individualism must be eradicated in the name of the common good. One wonders how many more people must be enslaved or eradicated by the ideologues and activists who lead revolutions, or take hold of governments, based on these discredited and provably inhuman dogmas. Of course, this is not to argue, and I do not argue, that the opposite is much better, such as the rule of the mob, the rule of the jungle, anarchy, etc. And I am aware of no society that is organized around such beliefs, as it is neither a society nor organized. The chaos that is modern Haiti comes to mind, where there is no law but the rule of a murderous mob. It is a relatively temporary condition that typically leads to some form of organized autocracy. As John Locke has informed us, this is also a primary reason why people enter in a social contract (civil society), to protect themselves and their property and develop rules and social norms.

What, then, is a working definition of liberty or at least a worthy understanding of the meaning of liberty for the purpose of better understanding the character of power?

Aristotle, who had a significant influence on America's Founders, references freedom often in his writings, but I do not find an explicit definition of the word. However, his meaning of liberty can be learned from his multiple explanations about it. Aristotle asserted that liberty is more than simply freedom to achieve an end. That would be bad liberty. Liberty must encourage virtue and discourage vice to fulfill man's spiritual needs. As for democracy, only a virtuous and moral people can successfully rule themselves. It is a view that was later shared by virtually every Founder who spoke on the subject. Aristotle also believed that a mixed regime—oligarchy and democracy—would best reflect such people, even though he was not a great admirer of democracy per se because he believed it had the potential to empower demagogues. It was left to Locke and Montesquieu, among others, to better flesh this out and, among other things, highlight the importance of dividing power into the three separate branches of government. Aristotle also emphasized that a government of laws not men (rulers) was more likely to ensure that sovereignty did not attach to the rulers.[1]

In 1748, Samuel Adams wrote an essay explicitly intended to define what was meant, or he meant, by liberty. He stated, in part:

> There is no one thing which mankind are more
> passionately fond of, which they fight with more

zeal for, which they possess with more anxious
jealousy and fear of losing, than liberty. But it has
fared with this, as with many other things, that
the true notion and just definition of it has been
but little understood, at the same time that zeal
for it and disputes about it have produced endless
altercations. There is certainly such a thing as
liberty, which distinguishes man from the beasts,
and a society of wise and reasonable creatures
from the brutal herd, where the strongest horns
are the strongest laws. And though the notions of
men were ten times more confused and unsettled,
and their opinions more various about this matter
than they are, there yet remains an internal and
essential distinction between this same liberty
and slavery.[2]

Next, Adams essentially summarizes Locke's explanation
of the state of nature:

In the state of nature, every man has a right to
think and act according to the dictates of his
own mind, which, in that state, are subject to no

other control and can be commanded by no other power than the laws and ordinances of the great Creator of all things. The perfection of liberty therefore, in a state of nature, is for every man to be free from any external force, and to perform such actions as in his own mind and conscience he judges to be Tightest; which liberty no man can truly possess whose mind is enthralled by irregular and inordinate passions; since it is no great privilege to be free from external violence if the dictates of the mind are controlled by a force within, which exerts itself above reason.[3]

But Adams writes that this state of nature alone is not enough to secure man's liberty. It is the foundation, but there must be more:

And had mankind continued in that innocent and happy state in which the sacred writings represent them as first created, it is possible that this liberty would have enjoyed in such perfection as to have rendered the embodying into civil society and the security of human laws altogether needless.[4]

Adams then turns to the type of government that best ensures liberty:

> The two main provisions by which a certain share in the government is secured to the people are their Parliaments and their juries; by the former of which no laws can be made without their consent, and by the latter none can be executed without their judgment. By the means the subject can never be oppressed by bad laws, nor lose the security of good ones, but by his own fault; . . . I will venture to assert that every man's security and happiness is much safer in such hands than under an arbitrary or aristocratical form of government. Especially since, but the wise provisions of our ancestors, both these powers are of short continuance; for power entrusted for a short time is not so likely to be perverted as that which is perpetual.[5]

There is not much to quibble with here. Adams is right about the preference for democracy over autocracy. But if you are looking for something akin to an actual definition of liberty, even though that was to be the subject of his essay, you will not find it.

As Adams himself would soon conclude, as one of the earliest and most effective revolutionaries against the British government he had once advocated for, even the best forms of government can devolve into tyrannies. Democracies do not guarantee liberty. They can provide the institutional framework for a humane government. And that institutional framework requires certain essential characteristics—a just rule of law, representation and consent, divided powers, private property rights—and a virtuous and moral people. However, liberty is not a product of democracy.

In Chapter 5, I discussed rights in relation to power. Yet it is impossible to discuss rights without the overlay of liberty, or the lack of liberty. Hence, there are numerous references to liberty in that chapter. When the Declaration of Independence speaks of "unalienable rights" it is talking about "life, liberty, and the pursuit of happiness." To take it a step further, by life, liberty, and the pursuit of happiness the Founders were highlighting the essence of human existence—your right, as a child of God, to live, to be free, and to pursue what fulfills your being.

Adams and many others underscore the importance of

the right kind of collective power that creates a civil society and, subsequently, a just government, the purpose of both being to secure a good and moral life for the individual and the people. Still, we do not have a definition of liberty, only a description of how to try to safeguard it—ultimately, the application of positive power.

Let us turn to the main author of the Declaration, Thomas Jefferson. On April 4, 1819, in a letter to Isaac H. Tiffany, Jefferson wrote:

> Of liberty I would say that, in the whole plenitude of its extent, it is unobstructed action according to our will. But *rightful liberty is unobstructed action according to our will within limits drawn around us by the equal rights of others.* I do not add "within the limits of the law," because law is often but the tyrant's will, and always so when it violates the right of an individual.[6]

However, without the law, *a just law*, there is no order, not even in the civil society. In Jefferson's defense, however, it is not clear if he is writing in a more theoretical sense or asserting his position as a baseline, or in the context of politics and government. The latter would not be very logical, so I have to assume the former.

Jefferson made many profound observations and was a prolific writer. One such statement—"[t]he natural progress of things is for liberty to yield and government to gain ground"—is, I believe, as close to a truism as it gets, at least over time.[7] Obviously, there are times and places when governments surrender power. But that clearly is not its "natural" tendency, not even in democracies. Moreover, governments can act and have, in fact, acted to protect or expand the rights of individuals or the people generally by exercising positive power. Again, here Jefferson is talking about "the natural progress of things," that is, the rule, not the exceptions to it.

Looking elsewhere, on August 26, 1789, the French National Assembly issued the Declaration of Human and Civic Rights. Article 4 is similar to Jefferson's pronouncement that "rightful liberty is unobstructed action according to our will within limits drawn around us by the equal rights of others." It states:

ARTICLE 4: Liberty consists in being able to do anything that does not harm others: thus, the

exercise of the natural rights of every man has no
bounds other than those that ensure to the other
members of society the enjoyment of these same
rights. These bounds may be determined only
by Law.[8]

However, Article 5 acknowledges the need for law, albeit
strictly limited in application:

ARTICLE 5: The Law has the right to forbid only
those actions that are injurious to society. Nothing
that is not forbidden by Law may be hindered,
and no one may be compelled to do what the Law
does not ordain.[9]

Again, Jefferson would undoubtedly agree here. We know
this from his own long public service in several governmental positions, including as president. Indeed, Locke, one of
Jefferson's greatest intellectual influences, goes further. The
purpose of the law is to *promote* freedom:

So that, however it may be mistaken, the end of
law is not to abolish or restrain, but to preserve

and enlarge freedom: for in all the states of created
beings capable of laws, where there is no law,
there is no freedom: for liberty is, to be free from
restraint and violence from others; which cannot
be, where there is no law: but freedom is not, as
we are told, a liberty for every man to do what
he lists: (for who could be free, when every other
man's humor might domineer over him?) but a
liberty to dispose and order as he lists, his persons,
actions, possessions, and his whole property,
which the allowance of those laws under which he
is, and therein not to be subject to the arbitrary
will of another, but freely follow his own.[10]

In 1859, John Stuart Mill, in his book *On Liberty*, wrote
what became known as the Harm Principle:

The object of this Essay is to assert one very
simple principle, as entitled to govern absolutely
the dealings of society with the individual in
the way of compulsion and control, whether the
means used be physical force in the form of legal
penalties, or the moral coercion of public opinion.

That principle is, that the sole end for which mankind is warranted, individually or collectively, in interfering with the liberty of action of any of their number, is self-protection. *That the only purpose for which* power *can be rightfully exercised over any member of a civilized community, against his will, is to prevent harm to others.* His own good, either physical or moral, is not a sufficient warrant. He cannot rightfully be compelled to do or forbear because it will be better for him to do so, because it will make him happier, because, in the opinion of others, to do so would be wise, or even right. . . . The only part of the conduct of anyone, for which he is amenable to society, is that which concerns others. In the part which merely concerns himself, his independence is, of right, absolute. Over himself, over his own body and mind, the individual is sovereign.[11]

Mill was not the first to make this argument, but he was among the most prominent. Yet in the last chapter of *On Liberty*, Mill rationally explains, "The principles asserted in these pages must be more generally admitted as the basis for discussion of details, before a consistent application of them to all the various departments of government and morals can be attempted with any prospect of advantage. . . . I offer, not so much applications, as specimens of application; which may serve to bring into greater clearness the meaning and limits of the two maxims which together form the entire doctrine of this Essay and to assist the judgment in holding the balance between them, in the cases where it appears doubtful which of them is applicable to the case."[12]

What are his two maxims?

The maxims are, first, that the individual is not accountable to society for his actions, in so far as these concern the interests of no person but himself. Advice, instruction, persuasion, and avoidance by other people, if thought necessary by them for their own good, are the only measures by which society can justifiably express its dislike or disapprobation of his conduct. *Secondly, that for such actions as are prejudicial to the interests of others, the individual is accountable, and may be subjected either to social or to legal punishments,*

if society is of the opinion that one or the other is
requisite for its protection.[13] (Italics added.)

This book is not intended to be a review of Mill or his book, but the importance of both in the liberty debate over the last century and a half is undeniable. Yet his great effort at defining liberty, which is truly extraordinary, seems to be largely undone by a single sentence, his second maxim, which acknowledges the need for law but is ambiguous to the point of providing substantial negative power and political latitude for government to determine the balance between liberty and authority.

Then there was Isaiah Berlin, who in 1958 delivered a lecture at Oxford University, and later wrote a book, on what he called the Two Concepts of Liberty. I mention it because it has a wide embrace among scholars. Berlin creates two categories of liberty—one that emphasizes individual liberty or the liberty of the people, and another that emphasizes government's role in securing liberty for the individual or the people (but also creates the conditions for tyranny). He assigns the former the name "negative liberty," because it lacks external coercion (freedom from interference), and the latter "positive liberty," because the issue is what kind of control is placed on the individual and his freedom (limitations placed on the individual by the broader society or government).

Berlin writes that "there are at least two senses of the word [liberty] which few would deny to be central, or at least two criteria which determine whether a man or a nation or a group is free or not. The first, which I shall call the negative sense or criterion, is the answer to the question 'What is the area within which the subject—a person or group of persons—is left to do what they like without control by other persons?' The second is the answer to the question 'What is the source of control, when it exists, which can prevent someone from doing what he wishes?' To say that there is only one sense of the word 'freedom,' but two criteria for its determination seems to me merely a confusion, for the two questions seem genuinely different, even though the answers to them may overlap. . . ."[14]

Berlin then discusses at length the nuances of each category, effectively moving in and out of what I see as subcategories of both positive and negative liberty—that is, the degree to which one or the other secures, expands, or diminishes individual liberty.

Berlin essentially repackages most of what we understand to be liberty versus tyranny and the endless degrees to which one seems to grow or shrink at the hands of the other. Moreover, his concept of positive liberty has less to do with liberty and more to do with, in the first instance, power. In my view, it is more useful and accurate to take on the subject of power and its basic forms. Indeed, are not negative and positive liberty first and foremost about who or what exercises power or who or what does not? Is that not what Berlin leans on to explain negative and positive liberty?

The common thread in all of this, from Aristotle to today, is that liberty is one of those words and one of those ideas that are best defined by, first, what they are not, and second, in the context of other words and ideas, such as rights (of course, as explained in Chapter 5, liberty without rights is essentially meaningless), morality, and virtue.

Even in a mostly open and democratic society, liberty's permeance goes largely unnoticed unless and until it is believed to be imperiled. Even then, depending on the nature of the threat, it may be ignored, unnoticed, or tolerated. Conversely, tyranny, again depending on its nature, seems easier to comprehend. It can be oppressive, cruel, unfair, severe, physical, psychological, etc. and, therefore, more readily seen and felt.

But when we talk about liberty and rights, do we not

repeatedly and necessarily come back to the question of power? Even when acknowledging God-given unalienable rights and universal, eternal truths, is that not the power of God as opposed to the power of man and of man's government?

I believe this to be a crucial point. As I wrote several times earlier, power, rights, and liberty are intertwined. The issue is, when trying to understand them and unraveling them for purposes of analyzing them how should one approach it?

That said, I move on to further examine how liberty was perceived by another of America's most influential Founders, Alexander Hamilton. His notion about liberty and the role of government often conflicted with Jefferson's and Madison's. Indeed, it turns out that Hamilton is among the most popular, if not the most popular, Founder among those who today support a more centralized and activist government. There is good reason for this. Hence, the popularity of *Hamilton* the Broadway musical, especially with the elites in entertainment, media, and politics, and among most academicians.

In examining Hamilton, I begin with Madison, who wrote in *Federalist* No. 45:

> The powers delegated by the proposed
> Constitution to the federal government are few

and defined. Those which are to remain in the State governments are numerous and indefinite. The former will be exercised principally on external objects, as war, peace, negotiation and foreign commerce; with which the last the power of taxation will for the most part be connected. The powers reserved to the several States will extend to all objects which, in the ordinary course of affairs, concern the lives, liberties and properties of the people, and the internal order, improvement and prosperity of the State.[15]

This was the overwhelming view of those who drafted and ratified the Constitution. Obviously, Hamilton fought for the Constitution's ratification. Along with Madison and, to a lesser extent, John Jay, he wrote the pro-Constitution Federalist Papers. Nonetheless, it is important to recall that at the Constitutional Convention, Hamilton, according to Madison's notes on the proceedings, clearly demonstrated his affinity for a powerful central government. Consider that he proposed "[letting] one branch of the Legislature hold their places for life or at least during good behavior. Let the

Executive also be for life. He appealed to the feelings of the members present whether a term of seven years, would induce the sacrifices of private affairs which an acceptance of public trust would require, so as to ensure the services of the best Citizens. On this plan we should have in the Senate a permanent will, a weighty interest, which would answer essential purposes."[16] Hamilton's idea was quickly dropped as it had almost no support.

Professor Raoul Berger, in his book *Federalism: The Founders' Design*, did more than most to delve deeply into the matter of *implied* and, conversely, *expressed* powers, which is crucial to determining how much liberty actually exists within democracies. The exercise of implied powers is too frequently an abusive exercise in unauthorized power. "Central to the constitutional scheme was restriction of the federal government to few defined and limited powers, and assurances that the States' residuary powers would be inviolable."[17] He explains that in *Federalist* No. 33, it was Hamilton who sought to ease any concerns the states may have had that the Constitution was establishing a federal government that could reach outside its expressed powers. Hamilton wrote: "What is power but the ability or faculty of doing a thing? What is the ability to do a thing but the power of employing the *means* necessary to its execution? . . . What are the proper *means* of executing such power, but necessary and proper laws?"[18]

Madison stated, writes Berger, that the clause "gives no supplementary power. It only enables them to execute the delegated powers."[19] Moreover, this was the clear understanding in the state ratification conventions.[20]

The plain text of Article I, Section 8, Clause 18 of the Constitution, referred to as the Necessary and Proper Clause, states:

> To make all laws which shall be necessary and *proper for carrying into execution* the foregoing powers and all other powers vested by this Constitution in the Government of the United States.[21] (Italics added.)

Berger observes that "the records make plain that the necessary and proper clause was merely designed to specifically authorize the employment of *means* to effectuate, to carry into execution, granted powers, not to augment them; and they strongly read against the doctrine of implied powers. . . ."[22] To be clear, Congress was not granted discretionary power by way of implied power to legislate at will.

Despite Hamilton's assurances, he believed in an energetic central government, and he was doggedly committed to this end as a close confidant of President George Washington as Treasury secretary. Putting aside his eloquent defense of the Constitution during the crucial state ratification debates, it appears Hamilton had different intentions once the state legislatures adopted the document. For example, in 1791, at the request of Washington and in defense of the constitutionality of the proposed Bank of the United States—which was vehemently opposed by both Jefferson and Madison—Hamilton wrote, in part:

> It is not denied that there are *implied* as well as express powers, and that the former are as effectually delegated as the latter. And for the sake of accuracy, it shall be mentioned, that there is another class of powers, which may be properly denominated resting powers. . . . It is conceded that *implied powers* are to be considered as delegated equally with express ones.[23]
>
> . . . This restrictive interpretation of the

word necessary [the Necessary and Proper Clause] is also contrary to this sound maxim of construction, namely, that the powers contained in a constitution of government, especially those which concern the general administration of the affairs of a country, its finances, trade, defense, etc., *ought to be construed liberally in advancement of the public good.* This rule does not depend on the particular form of a government, or on the particular demarcation of the boundaries of its powers, but on the nature and object of government itself. The means by which national exigencies are to be provided for, national inconveniences obviated, national prosperity promoted, are of such infinite variety, extent, and complexity, that there must of necessity be great latitude of discretion in the selection and application of those means. Hence, consequently, the necessity and propriety of exercising the authorities entrusted to a government on principles of liberal construction. . . .[24]

It leaves, therefore, a criterion of what is constitutional, and of what is not so. This criterion is the end, to which the measure relates as a mean. If the end be clearly comprehended within any of the specified powers, and if the measure has an obvious relation to that end, and is not forbidden by any particular provision of the Constitution, it may safely be deemed to come within the compass of the national authority. There is also this further criterion, which may materially assist the decision: Does the proposed measure abridge a pre-existing right of any State or of any individual? If it does not, there is a strong presumption in favor of its constitutionality, and slighter relations to any declared object of the Constitution may be permitted to turn the scale.[25]

Hamilton argued for a tectonic shift away from the near-universal understanding of the Constitution's structure, which drew the strong ire of both Jefferson and Madison, among others. They argued that Congress had no power to create such a national bank. That it was the role of the states to create banks, if they so desired. They were furious with Hamilton's assertion of implied powers and his expansive reading of the Constitution.

In his 1791 letter to Washington arguing against the bank bill, Jefferson explained that Hamilton's interpretation of the Constitution "would reduce the whole instrument to a single phrase, that of instituting a Congress with power to do whatever would be for the good of the United States; and, as they would be the sole judges of the good or evil, it would be also a power to do whatever evil they please."[26] On the House floor, Madison insisted that Hamilton's proposal was "a broad construction of federal powers . . . [that would deliver] a powerful blow at the barriers against an indefinite expansion of federal authority."[27]

Thus, the debate over how to interpret the Constitution erupted early in the republic. And it would only get more intense. Not only would the *manner of interpretation* be disputed but also *who should interpret the Constitution and have the final say* would take a radically unexpected turn, with the 1803 Supreme Court *Marbury v. Madison* decision.

In that case, Chief Justice John Marshall wrote an infamous decision that would further alter the nature and character of the Constitution. Marshall declared, among other things, "It is emphatically the province and duty of the judicial department to say what the law is. Those who apply the rule to particular cases, must of necessity expound and interpret that rule." He later noted that the judicial power was extended to "all cases arising under the constitution." Therefore, Marshall concluded, it was "too extravagant to be maintained that the Framers had intended that a case arising under the constitution should be decided without examining the instrument under which it arises."[28]

Thus, judicial review was born, a phrase and power that is not in the Constitution, through an implied power created and applied by the Supreme Court itself. Shortly after Congress's power had been significantly expanded, the court went even further by seizing ultimate and final authority for itself. The centralization of governmental power began in earnest.

It is no coincidence that both Hamilton and Marshall were partisan members of the Federalist Party. Although Hamilton despised John Adams, also a Federalist, and Adams nominated Marshall to chief justice, who was quickly confirmed by the lame-duck Federalist Congress, their view of government was similar enough and conflicted significantly with Jefferson, Madison, and their Democratic-Republican Party.

The matter of liberty, and its application to the future of the country, was dramatically changed from the original understanding of those who drafted, adopted, and ratified the Constitution, and its exquisitely elaborate distribution of power, to the implied and expansive view of power held by a small minority of politicians at the time. The primary lawmakers were to be the states. Indeed, it is highly unlikely that if a constitution of this sort had actually been drafted and submitted to the state conventions, it would have been ratified.

Moreover, the extraordinary claim and assertion of power by the Supreme Court to make final declarations about constitutional disputes, which was not conferred on the court by the Constitution and was never seriously contemplated (indeed, the ratifying state conventions were assured the judiciary would be the weakest branch), altered the balance of power set out in the Constitution and contemplated by its signatories. In the United States today, the people, and often the branches of government, are expected to comply with court orders even when these orders arguably defy the Constitution. In such cases, the judges are honored and the Constitution is not.

Although there are avenues for Congress to rein in the courts, it is difficult to accomplish. The impeachment of judges is impracticable, as it requires a supermajority of senators to convict. The elimination of judges through the power of the purse, in a process called budget reconciliation, seems possible since it avoids a Senate filibuster. However, even this depends on whether the matter is considered as primarily a budget or policy matter, in which the Senate parliamentarian plays an interpretative role. Congress can remove jurisdictional authority from the courts, but this proposition could also face a Senate filibuster. It is easier for a judge to exercise authority he does not have than to remove him for his ill-gotten authority. Moreover, when the problem rests not with one judge but dozens or scores of them, the response becomes more complicated and difficult. This is not to say that Congress should choose inaction, but whatever path is chosen will be difficult. Nonetheless, it is imperative.

Of course, there are those who celebrate the centralization of government decision-making, the empowerment of the ruling class, and the dismembering of representative government. They often assemble a list of economic and social accomplishments instituted by the federal government in defense of it amassing power, including, for example, the abolition of slavery, the right of women to vote, the civil rights movement, etc. But their rendition of history is often disingenuous. They ignore the role the federal government played in retaining slavery, such as the Fugitive Slave Acts and the Supreme Court's *Dred Scott* decision, and the plurality of states that opposed slavery and, after the Civil War, enacted the Thirteenth, Fourteenth, and Fifteenth Amendments. The women's suffrage movement was organized by private citizens before the Civil War and originally had nothing to do with the federal government (not until 1920 was the Nineteenth Amendment ratified, by three-fourths of the *states*); and the civil rights movement was first launched by churches and social organizations through nonviolent protests, not by the federal or state governments. And what of the internment of Japanese Americans during World War II, the rampant racism of the Wilson administration, or the attack on a free press with the Sedition Act by John Adams and later Woodrow Wilson?* The list is much longer, but good enough for illustrative purposes.

To be clear, my point is not that states are all good and that the federal government is all bad, as there are countless examples to the contrary. Only a fool would suggest either.

---

* Incidentally, in 1940, President Franklin Roosevelt refused to sign bipartisan legislation outlawing lynching; for more about his failure to address racial inequality, see *The Democrat Party Hates America*.

Both have done terrible things and great things. Rather, it is clear that the attempt, often by politicians and academicians, who are driven more by progressive ideology than adherence to the Constitution, is to justify ratcheting up ever-more-centralized governmental and nonconsensual power and characterizing it in positive-power terms—as exclusively gifting and securing rights and liberties. The deceptive and manipulative propaganda that encourages disfiguring the constitutional construct is a dangerous gambit. Indeed, virtually any despot can be said to have done something beneficial for a country. Yet if the celebration of centralized government is not the monopoly view of the Democrat Party, the media, and academia, it is certainly their overwhelmingly held view. They also seek their agenda through an activist reinterpretation of the Constitution, not amendment processes in which they would surely fail.

Critics are right to ask: Exactly what do the negative-power advocates seek to achieve and why are they not explicit about it? Of course, some are, but I am not speaking here of the more fanatical and openly hostile among them. My focus is on those politicians and academicians who claim to embrace and uphold the Constitution while using it, by manipulation and perversion, as a means to dismember its most critical parts, especially separation of powers, the consent of the people, and federalism. What is their practical governing blueprint? And how does it advance the cause of individual and societal liberty?

It is only the Constitution's remaining yet weakened barriers against negative power that protect us from the logical progression of an increasingly centralized government with an authoritarian ruling class—that is, authoritarian democracy. Ultimately, this is the problem with a Hamiltonian-Marshall view. As time goes on, precedent is built upon precedent, as the outer limits of these abuses are tested and pushed, and the barriers slowly atrophy. The system becomes less constitutional and more imperious.

Of course, state and local governments, even homeowners' associations, are subject to kindred abuses and malfeasances—where an individual might be driven to leave the state, town, or development for a better life elsewhere. But mobility is not an easy or realistic answer for most when the power-hungry impose their will nationwide by a central government that rules supreme over the other governing entities and escape involves leaving the country. Again, this assumes that the constitutional barriers against such tyranny have been largely usurped.

It bears repeating, the Constitution is constructed around America's founding principles, as concisely and formally proclaimed in the Declaration of Independence. These are to be the guiding principles for government and governance. The progressive glorification and even deification of centralized authority—whether in courts, an executive, or a legislature—, in the end, is antithetical to liberty* and the sovereignty of the people. And even in this, they favor such centralization and exercise of negative power only when it expands *their* authority and promotes *their* governing ideology.

I have spent considerable time in this chapter discussing Hamilton, albeit truncated, and, to a lesser extent, Marshall. I have also discussed Wilson's ideas in various chapters. Although important on their own for the purposes of this book, the journey, or should I say trajectory, from the Federalists Hamilton and Marshall to the progressive Wilson and American Marxism of today illustrates the steady rise of negative power over positive power even in the most carefully designed governmental system. I believe it can be said with some confidence that today Hamilton would identify more with the progressives than their opposites, even though

---

* By *liberty* here I mean true liberty as contemplated and intended, and variously defined, by those with good and honest intentions.

he not only voted for the Constitution as a delegate from New York, but as previously mentioned, brilliantly campaigned for it in the Federalist Papers. However, I do not believe Hamilton would ascribe to the most radical cultural and amoral parts of the progressive ideology or stand with its more extreme members. Despite his enthusiasm for centralized government, I find no ideological commitment to dismantle the Constitution in pursuit of some ideological fiction or fantasy.

Of course, much more can be written about liberty, as it can be about rights and, indeed, power. But much will be achieved if what has been written leads to further inquiry— and a public more alert to the dangers of tyranny disguised or presented as rights and liberty. The best way to understand them is how they are to be applied through power or how power is to be applied to them.

EPILOGUE

There is much more that can be said about power than not. As I mentioned earlier in the book, it is more than a word or a simple descriptor. Indeed, understanding power has been an intellectual pursuit of philosophers for thousands of years, most notably Plato, Aristotle, Cicero, Hobbes, Locke, Spinoza, Montesquieu, Schopenhauer, Nietzsche, and scores more. If they did not try to tackle it directly, they incorporated it into their observations about related ideas and subjects.

By one account, the word *power* appears 263 times in the Bible, with 40 important Bible scriptures on power.[1]

Power dynamics are truly everywhere—at home, in the workplace, in social circles, in faith, etc. But the focus of this book is the relationship and exercise of power in society, politics, and government, and its role in securing or destroying our liberty and rights. While intellectuals and writers may discuss power at length, it is not commonly understood, let alone appreciated by most as central to their lives.

There are a limitless number of areas I considered pursuing in this book, such as power and education, power and equality, power and immigration, power and wealth, and so on. But there are practical limits to how many topics can be explored in the context of one book without it becoming overwhelming to the reading audience on whom I am focused. The purpose of this book, and the manner in which I have addressed and pursued this topic, is to spur interest and thought where it may not have previously existed, and to lay a modest foundation from which others can begin their own journey.

NOTES

1: On Power

1. Collected Works of Abraham Lincoln, vol. 7 (November 5, 1863–September 12, 1864), *Collected Works of Abraham Lincoln*, University of Michigan Library Digital Collections. To underscore the point, evil is often cloaked in liberty, and not only in autocratic regimes but from elements within democracies that do not accept or honor the limits democratic institutions place on power but instead exploit them and abuse them in the name of liberty.
2. George Orwell, *Politics and the English Language,* http://public-library.uk/ebooks/72/30.pdf, 5.
3. Ibid.
4. Vanessa A. Boese, "State of the World 2021: Autocratization Changing Its Nature,"

Democratization, March 30, 2022, https://www
.tandfonline.com/doi/full/10.1080/13510347.2022
.2069751#abstract.

5. National Archives, "The Constitution: How Did It
Happen," https://www.archives.gov/founding-docs
/constitution/how-did-it-happen.

6. Charles Montesquieu, *The Spirit of the Laws*
(Cambridge: Cambridge University Press, 1989),
155–56 (emphasis added).

7. C. S. Lewis, *God in the Dock: Essays on Theology and
Ethics* (Grand Rapids, MI: Eerdmans, 1970).

8. Montesquieu, *The Spirit of the Laws,* 157.

9. James Madison, *Federalist* No. 51, Dawson, ed.,
https://en.wikisource.org/wiki/The_Federalist
_(Dawson)/51.

2: On Negative Power

1. Ludwig von Mises, *Marxism Unmasked: From Delusion
to Destruction* (Foundation for Economic Freedom,
2006), https://fee.org/ebooks/marxism-unmasked
-from-delusion-to-destruction/.

2. See Woodrow Wilson, "July 4, 1914: Fourth of July
Address," University of Virginia Miller Center, https://

millercenter.org/the-presidency/presidential-speeches
/july-4-1914-fourth-july-address.

3. Richard A. Posner, "Enlightened Despot," *New Republic*, April 23, 2007, https://newrepublic.com
/article/60919/enlightened-despot.

4. Ibid.

5. Alexis de Tocqueville, *Democracy in America* (New York: Knopf, 1994), 318–19.

6. Ibid.

7. Ibid.

8. Ibid.

9. Marshall Hargrave, "What Is Supranational? Definition, Criticism, and Example," *Investopedia*, March 3, 2025, https://www.investopedia.com/terms
/s/supranational.asp.

10. Eleanor Stratton quoting John Adams, "Founders' Vision of Virtuous Citizenry," USConstitution.net, June 12, 2024, https://www.usconstitution.net
/founders-vision-of-virtuous-citizenry/.

11. Ibid., quoting George Washington.

12. Ibid., quoting James Madison.

3: On Positive Power

1. Mark R. Levin, *Liberty and Tyranny* (New York: Threshold Editions, 2009), 14.

2. Thank You For Praying, "Exploring the Similarities Between Judaism and Christianity," https://thankyouforpraying.com/judaism-and-christianity-similarities/.

3. U.S. Const. Amend. 1 § 1.

4. *Thomas Jefferson: Writings*, ed. Merrill D. Peterson (New York: Library of America, 1984), 1500–1501; "Letter to Henry Lee," https://americanfounding.org/entries/letter-to-henry-lee/.

5. Steve Postal, "Muslim Reformer Discusses Middle East Peace, Islamist Terror in Europe: An Interview with Dr. M. Zuhdi Jasser," *American Spectator*, December 7, 2020, https://spectator.org/middle-east-peace-islamist-terror-interview-m-zuhdi-jasser/.

6. Marilyn Stern, "Zuhdi Jasser on Viewing Islam Through 'the Lens of Liberty and Enlightenment,'" Middle East Forum, October 16, 2020, https://www.meforum.org/jasser-on-islam-liberty-and-enlightenment.

7. Alexis de Tocqueville, *Democracy in America*, 4th ed., vol. 2 (New York: Langley, 1841), 23.

8. Postal, "Muslim Reformer Discusses Middle East Peace, Islamist Terror in Europe."

9. Dr. M. Zuhdi Jasser, *A Battle for the Soul of Islam* (New York: Threshold Editions, 2012), 219.

10. Ibid., 219–20.

11. Ibid., 220.

12. Raymond Ibrahim, "How Taqiyya Alters Islam's Rules of War," *Middle East Quarterly*, Winter 2010, vol. 17, no. 1.

13. Karl Marx, "A Contribution to the Critique of Hegel's Philosophy of Right," *Works of Karl Marx 1843*, https://www.marxists.org/archive/marx/works/1843/critique-hpr/intro.htm.

14. Ibid. (emphasis added).

15. Ibid.

16. Ibid.

4: On Language

1. Britannica, "agitprop," *Britannica.com*, https://www.britannica.com/topic/agitprop, April 16, 2025.

2. Ibid.

3. Hannah Arendt, *The Origins of Totalitarianism* (New York: Mariner Books, 1968), 344.

4. Ibid., 345.

5. Ibid., 346.

6. Ludwig von Mises, *Marxism Unmasked: From Delusion to Destruction* (Foundation for Economic Freedom, 2006), https://fee.org/ebooks/marxism-unmasked -from-delusion-to-destruction/.

7. James Lindsay, "The Complex Relationship Between Marxism and Wokeness," *New Discourses*, July 28, 2020, https://newdiscourses.com/2020/07/complex -relationship-between-marxism-wokeness/.

8. U.S. Const. Art. V.

9. Ibid.

10. Just Security, "Litigation Tracker: Legal Challenges to Trump Administration Actions," May 3, 2025, https:// www.justsecurity.org/107087/tracker-litigation-legal -challenges-trump-administration/.

11. Senator Charles Schumer, "Schumer Defends Voting with GOP Saying Shutdown Would Be Worse," *PBS News Hour*, March 19, 2025, https://www.pbs.org/news hour/show/we-had-an-awful-choice-schumer -defends-voting-with-gop-saying-shutdown-would-be -worse.

12. Charles Montesquieu, *The Spirit of the Laws* (Cambridge: Cambridge University Press, 1989), 157.

13. Raoul Berger, *Government by Judiciary* (Carmel, CA: Liberty Fund, 1997), 323.

14. "Differences in Ideas of Marx and Hegel," *Political Science*, https://www.politicalsciencenotes.com /marxism/differences-in-ideas-of-marx-and-hegel /1237.

15. J. V. Stalin, *Constitution (Fundamental Law) of the Union of Soviet Socialist Republics* (London: Red Star Press, 1978), Marxist Internet Archive, 2008, https:// www.marxists.org/reference/archive/stalin/works/1936 /12/05.htm.

16. Norman M. Naimark, "Stalin's Genocides," Hoover Institution, January 12, 2011, https://www.hoover.org /research/stalins-genocides.

17. Yongyi Song, "Chronology of Mass Killings During the Chinese Cultural Revolution (1966–1976)," SciencesPo, August 25, 2011, https://www.sciencespo .fr/mass-violence-war-massacre-resistance/en/document /chronology-mass-killings-during-chinese-cultural -revolution-1966-1976.html.

18. Olivia Enos, Anouk Wear, and Sophie Richardson, "Prioritizing Human Rights in United States Policy Toward China: A Guide for the Trump Administration," Hudson Institute, January 28, 2025, https://www.hudson.org/human-rights/prioritizing -human-rights-us-policy-toward-china-guide-trump -administration-olivia-enos.

19. Ronald Radosh, "Bernie's Adventures on a Stalinist Kibbutz," Hudson Institute, February 6, 2016, https:// www.hudson.org/domestic-policy/bernie-s-adventures -on-a-stalinist-kibbutz.

20. Tax Foundation, "Tax Reduction and Reform: A Summary of President Kennedy's Tax Proposals," February 11, 1963, https://taxfoundation.org/research /all/federal/tax-reduction-and-reform-summary -president-kennedys-tax-proposals/.

21. Tax Foundation, "Retrospective on the 1981 Reagan Tax Cut," June 10, 2004, https://taxfoundation.org /research/all/federal/retrospective-1981-reagan-tax-cut/.

22. Charlotte Nickerson, "Mere Exposure Effect in Psychology: Biases & Heuristics," *Simply Psychology*, October 10, 2023, https://www.simplypsychology.org /mere-exposure-effect.html.

23. Mark R. Levin, *Rediscovering Americanism* (New York: Threshold Editions, 2017), 119–20.

5: On Rights

1. National Archives, U.S. Declaration of Independence, https://www.archives.gov/founding-docs/declaration-transcript.

2. National Archives, Virginia Declaration of Rights, https://www.archives.gov/founding-docs/virginia-declaration-of-rights.

3. James Madison, *Federalist* No. 51, Dawson, ed., https://en.wikisource.org/wiki/The_Federalist_(Dawson)/51.

4. See Mark R. Levin, *Rediscovering Americanism* (New York: Threshold Editions, 2017), chap. 1.

5. James Madison, *The Papers of James Madison*, ed. William T. Hutchinson et al. (Chicago: University of Chicago Press, 1962); also in *The Founders' Constitution* (Chicago: University of Chicago Press), vol. 1, chap. 16, doc. 23, https://press-pubs.uchicago.edu/founders/documents/v1ch16s23.html.

6. Larry P. Arnn, *The Founders' Key* (Nashville: Nelson Books, 2013), 23–24.

7. Karl Marx, *Manifesto of the Communist Party*, chap. II, https://www.marxists.org/archive/marx/works/1848/communist-manifesto/ch02.htm.

8. Ibid.

9. Friedrich Engels, "Withering Away of the State," *The Encyclopedia of Political Science*, ed. George Thomas Kurian (CQ Press, 2010), https://sk.sagepub.com/ency/edvol/the-encyclopedia-of-political-science/chpt/withering-away-the-state.

10. Robert A. Berman, "At 200, Marx Is Still Wrong," Hoover Institution, May 15, 2018, https://www.hoover.org/research/200-marx-still-wrong.

11. Ibid.

12. Ibid.

13. Franklin Delano Roosevelt, "The Economic Bill of Rights," January 11, 1944, USHistory.org, https://www.ushistory.org/documents/economic_bill_of_rights.htm (emphasis added).

14. Frédéric Bastiat, *The Law* (New York: The Foundation for Economic Education, 1950), 8–9.

15. John Majewski, "How the Industrial Revolution Raised the Quality of Life for Workers and Their

Families," Foundation for Economic Freedom, July 1, 1986, https://fee.org/resources/the-industrial-revolution-working-class-poverty-or-prosperity/.

16. George Reisman, *Capitalism* (Ottawa, IL: Jameson Books, 1996), 76–77.

17. Thomas Paine, *Common Sense* (1776), Online Library of Liberty, https://oll.libertyfund.org/pages/1776-paine-common-sense-pamphlet.

6: On Liberty

1. See Moira M. Walsh, "Aristotle's Conception of Freedom," *Journal of the History of Philosophy* 35, no. 4 (1997): 495–507, Project MUSE, https://dx.doi.org/10.1353/hph.1997.0081.

2. Samuel Adams, "Definition of Liberty," National Center for the Development of Constitutional Strategies, https://ncdcs.org/the-tale-of-two-constitutions/definition-of-liberty/.

3. Ibid.

4. Ibid.

5. Ibid.

6. Thomas Jefferson, "Thomas Jefferson to Isaac H.

Tiffany, 4 April 1819," Founders Online, https://founders.archives.gov/documents/Jefferson/03-14-02-0191 (emphasis added).

7. Edward Dumbauld, ed., *The Political Writings of Thomas Jefferson* (New York: Liberal Arts Press, 1955), 138.

8. Conseil Constitutionelle (French Constitutional Council), "Declaration of Human and Civic Rights of 26 August 1789," https://www.conseil-constitutionnel.fr/sites/default/files/as/root/bank_mm/anglais/cst2.pdf.

9. Ibid.

10. John Locke, *Two Treatises of Government* (London: Witmore & Fenn, 1821), 234.

11. John Stuart Mill, *On Liberty* (Oxford, 1859), 21–22.

12. Ibid., 100.

13. Ibid. (emphasis added).

14. Isaiah Berlin, "Two Concepts of Liberty," in *Four Essays on Liberty* (Oxford: Oxford University Press, 1969), http://fs2.american.edu/dfagel/www/Philosophers/Berlin/Berlin_twoconceptsofliberty.pdf.

15. James Madison, *Federalist* No. 45, Dawson, ed., https://en.wikisource.org/wiki/The_Federalist_(Dawson)/45.

16. Gaillard Hunt and James Brown Scott, eds., *The Debates in the Federal Convention of 1787 Which Framed the Constitution of the United States of America. Reported by James Madison*, Founders Online, https://founders.archives.gov/documents/Hamilton/01-04-02-0098-0003#ARHN-01-04-02-0098-0003-fn-0014.

17. Raoul Berger, *Federalism: The Founders' Design* (Norman: University of Oklahoma Press, 1987), 88.

18. Ibid.

19. Ibid., 89.

20. Ibid.

21. U.S. Const., Art. I, § 8, cl. 18.

22. Berger, *Federalism*, 95–96 (emphasis added).

23. Alexander Hamilton, *The Federalist: A Commentary on the Constitution of the United States by Alexander Hamilton, James Madison and John Jay* (New York: Henry Holt, 1898); "Hamilton's Opinion as to the Constitutionality of the Bank of the United States: 1791," Avalon Project, Yale Law School, https://avalon.law.yale.edu/18th_century/bank-ah.asp (emphasis added).

24. Ibid. (emphasis added).

25. Ibid.

26. *Letter from Thomas Jefferson to George Washington on the Constitutionality of the Bank of the United States, 1791*, http://www.pasleybrothers.com/mocourses/texts/Jefferson_on_BUS.htm.

27. Scot Bomboy, "Hamilton's Treasury Department and a Great Constitutional Debate," National Constitution Center, September 2, 2020, https://constitutioncenter.org/blog/hamiltons-treasury-department-and-a-great-constitutional-debate.

28. *Marbury v. Madison*, 5 U.S. 137 (1803).

Epilogue

1. https://connectusfund.org/40-important-bible-scriptures-on-power.